TO MARIJANA
ENJOY MY
STORY

4ᵗ AUG 2013

Circumstances
Unforeseen

Alan Springall

BALBOA
PRESS

A DIVISION OF HAY HOUSE

Balboa Press books may be ordered through booksellers or by contacting:

Balboa Press
A Division of Hay House
1663 Liberty Drive
Bloomington, IN 47403
www.balboapress.com
1-(877) 407-4847

ISBN: 978-1-4525-4395-6 (sc)
ISBN: 978-1-4525-4396-3 (hc)
ISBN: 978-1-4525-4394-9 (e)

Library of Congress Control Number: 2011962325

Because of the dynamic nature of the Internet, any web addresses or
links contained in this book may have changed since publication and
may no longer be valid. The views expressed in this work are solely those
of the author and do not necessarily reflect the views of the publisher,
and the publisher hereby disclaims any responsibility for them.

The author of this book does not dispense medical advice or prescribe the use
of any technique as a form of treatment for physical, emotional, or medical
problems without the advice of a physician, either directly or indirectly. The
intent of the author is only to offer information of a general nature to help
you in your quest for emotional and spiritual well-being. In the event you use
any of the information in this book for yourself, which is your constitutional
right, the author and the publisher assume no responsibility for your actions.

Any people depicted in stock imagery provided by Thinkstock are
models, and such images are being used for illustrative purposes only.
Certain stock imagery © Thinkstock.

Printed in the United States of America

Balboa Press rev. date: 03/30/2012

Foreword

This is the recipe for this great story and the recollections of a simpler time.

An elderly chap seeking a last fling at enjoying life.

A man on a tight budget and a mission to gain or use funds from as many banks as possible while enroute across Europe.

A foreign car that that would not run well and consistently needed repairs

Camping out in tents and using canned foods in an effort to cut costs

A long journey across Europe by car.

My first attempt at this story was in 1990. I had made many attempts since then but I could not generate much motivation to continue. interest. Not being an English literature scholar, confidence to write was not on my side. This is written in very plain simple English. My journal notes were not extensive but enough to jog my memory into putting together this story.

Many things would have changed if I where to retrace the journey again.

I would most certainly have extensive service done on the vehicle at a certified automotive dealer.

The vehicle chosen would have air-conditioning and would have all the modern extras and stick shift.

It would also be a camper van for comfort.

Knowing where all the campsites were and their facilities plus space available would be known (G P S and internet) and be a great time saver.

In today's world of modern technology camping I'm sure would be very different from when we camped in 1976. I would aim to eliminate as many of the problems we encountered as possible. The whole financial situation in this day and age would be very different.

Acknowledgements and Dedication

My wife who had to put up with my total dedication for over one year working on the story evenings, weekends, and whenever I had a spare hour.

A very big thank you to my lovely mother who told me to apply for the job of driving the gentleman and having this great adventure.

Also in memory of my late father and son who would have enjoyed my story.

A retired school teacher who encouraged me to actually go ahead with the story after I told him of the adventure. This was after I told him this story while we shared a cabana on a beach in Mexico.

A woman and unknown yet very experienced editor, who completed the very first extensive edit of this work.

Thanks also to a very enthusiastic neighbour who had an excellent knowledge of English communications and spent countless hours helping me with the rewrites of the entire story. Also to an older friend who read my first manuscript and also advised me on some very important details.

Thanks to my friends, neighbours and co-workers who cheered me on.

These people encouraged me to share this riveting story and helped me push on and meet the deadlines.

CIRCUMSTANCES UNFORESEEN

I was born in Winchester, England in 1951 to English parents who raised me with a good British discipline in a working class environment. I have one brother.

My mother's maiden name was of French descent (Bevis: Bovis in French) from over one hundred years ago. Her grandfather had a fishing fleet, so we have a certain amount of seafaring blood in us. My mother was a housekeeper to a wealthy chain store owner and also picked strawberries to help support the family income.

My father worked at British Aerospace making fuel tanks for passenger airliners. He had an Irish mother and an English father, a Cockney who was born within the sound of "bo bells" in downtown London He served in the Welsh Regiment and was one of the sharp shooter of his regiment during World War one. He was a perfect shot with a rifle

My younger brother was a boatyard manager who took care of expensive

Yachts, hauling them out with a Renner boat hoist (a machine much like a giant four poster bed with wheels on the corners). He would store them in the fall, and launch them in the spring.

In August 1967, my working career began as an apprentice boat builder and after completing a 5 year apprenticeship I moved on and built catamarans for a number of years. I spent seven years in the exhibition and display business. On one occasion, I travelled to Malaysia for the Asian Defence Exhibition. I became a life insurance salesman (not a great success, the company went bankrupt), and I worked on suspended ceilings for a contractor in southern England.

Returning to carpentry, I found fascinating and challenging jobs in furniture restoration and home repair. I was then working in my own business and subcontracting for a local builder.

During my seven year marriage I had one son, who was now driving a delivery truck and was installing double—glazing in the London area. This was a surprise, because he had played in Oliver at the London Palladium, and he was an excellent dancer and actor. I had expected him to take up an acting career. Sadly he died in a car accident at the age 24 in May 2006.

Opportunity called and I was offered a job building boats near Toronto, Ontario. When I arrived in Toronto, Canada, I lived with a friend at Kingston Road and Queen Street. This was not a comfortable arrangement as I could not pay my way, and I wanted to have some independence and privacy. After finding a job with a closet company, I then found other accommodations. I worked for the closet company for six and a half years. I became their production manager, but the company was sold and I moved over to the new company. After eight months, my job was made redundant.

I was not having much success in finding work, and after sending out many resumes, I completed a computer course. I sold vacuum cleaners for a short time. My next venture was selling Ford cars and trucks at a local dealership for a year. That too, did not last long.

I worked at a large manufacturing company as a night supervisor for their office manufacturing division. I would start at 4:30 pm and finish at 12:30 am. This allowed me the time during the day to write.

This did not last long as I was transferred to the day shift working from seven-thirty to four-thirty in the afternoon. I was now working as a receiver for the work surfaces section and dealing with two suppliers. Time was not on my side to write, so again, I lost interest, as I had no spare time in which to continue with the book. I worked next as the Health and Safety Coordinator for the company. This involved a lot of training and supervision. Now the hours were a bit more to my liking. This allowed me to complete some writing in the mornings, before starting work at seven-thirty.

This is my story of a journey across Europe that I made in 1976 with an elderly gentleman, who said he was an artist who wanted one last jaunt before he would be unable to travel. Since he would soon retire, he wanted to drive to Singapore. However with his eyesight failing, he wanted to do some nice paintings en route, while he was still able.

His plan was to camp to cut costs, since he was on a small budget. He purchased a 1966 Ford Comet for this trip abroad. It proved to be a real problem as this was not the best vehicle for such a lengthy journey. Major repairs in Europe would slow down our trip and "eat" at his finances.

The journey involved three of us; the third person came along as a paying passenger to help with the cost of gas. I was not aware, until I arrived back in the UK many weeks later, that the elderly gentleman was wanted by the police.

I kept a daily journal during my travel adventure and what follows is a true description of that summertime journey.

CHAPTER 1

After losing my fiancée to another man, I was very depressed and did not have much interest in anything. My life insurance business was not enough to keep me occupied. My doctor prescribed some anti-depressants; however I couldn't seem to get my life back on track.

Then one very hot day, feeling low and depressed, I took a couple of pills and tried to go to sleep. This did not work, so I proceeded to work in my parents' garden thinking this would expend some energy and make me tired, so I could relax and maybe go to sleep later in the afternoon.

My neighbour saw me and wondered what I was doing, working at such an alarming rate, in the scorching heat of the day.

After doing a huge amount of work, I became very thirsty, and went into the house for a drink. I was unaware that the heat exhaustion and dehydration had taken effect. The telephone rang and I answered it. Whoever it was, could not understand me because my speech had become very slurred.

My parents were visiting their friends, and for some reason, my dad decided to come home instead of staying late for a drink. This was a very unusual decision for him to make as he never refused a drink with his old school pal, Gordon.

They arrived at our door just as I was trying to answer the phone, but I was on the floor and it was very difficult for them to get in. Dad took the phone from me and spoke to whoever it was on the other end. He then called my mother's brother from next door to carry me into the front room, and to help put me on the couch.

They called an ambulance, not knowing what was wrong with me. Mom came in the ambulance with me and the attendant quizzed her to find out all he could so as to relate to the emergency staff what action to take. I was not coherent during all this, and was rolling the attendant's sleeve up and down as he was carefully restraining me. I have no recollection of the events that followed, just what my mother told me afterwards.

It was quite a night in the hospital, and, I was not allowed to go to sleep for a very long time, as the nurse kept waking me up and asking my name and where I came from. It was not until morning that I was left alone to sleep in peace. When I awoke later that evening, there was a gentleman sitting by my bed; he asked me how I was feeling, and told me he had to ask me some of questions as to what happened.

The long sleep had brought me back to the reality of what had happened. I told him that I felt fine and he proceeded to tell me that it was very dangerous to take any drugs of this nature and work in the heat.

My ex-fiancée came to see me. This was a real surprise, as we had broken up some weeks before. I thanked her for thinking of me, but told her I did not want to see her again. Being a nurse in the hospital, she probably found out that I was there.

Later that evening, my dad came to take me home. My father, as strict as he was, did not ask me any questions about the incident. It was tough but I persuaded him to come with me to the nurses' quarters to retrieve my engagement ring,

She was not surprised, especially since I had already told her that I did not want to see her any more. She gave the ring up without any fuss. We left the hospital and all my father would talk about was business. He was very sure that with my carpentry skills, there would be many things I could do. It was great to get back home, and was as if a huge weight had been lifted off me. I had listened very intently to my father all the way home and decided that he was right, and I should venture back into carpentry.

As a carpenter, I looked in the paper every day but did not see any jobs that interested me. However, what I did see was that that a driver was wanted to drive an artist to Singapore. This was a very appealing premise, as I loved adventure and travel.

When I spoke to my mother about it, she said, "Apply if you think you would like to do that. You have nothing to lose, many people will apply but someone has to get the job."

The advertisement only gave a post office box number to apply to. After writing a long letter explaining why it would be the perfect job for me, I drove to Southampton to take my application directly to the newspaper. I drove home confident that my chance of getting this job was good. Having gone through such turmoil over the past few weeks, my spirits were now more positive.

CHAPTER 2

Five days after posting my letter, the phone rang, and it was the man who had placed the advertisement. All this time, my mom said "don't worry he probably has many replies, and is taking his time going through them."

The man's name was Brian Turner. He told me that 126 men had applied for the position. He was going to read and re-read all the letters then phone all those who he thought would be most suitable for the job. After doing this, he would make a short list of 26 and interview all of them. Should he decide to put me on that list, he would call me again for a meeting. A week went by, and then I got a call asking me to see him at his house. It began to get interesting, because I felt I had a good chance of getting the job.

He lived in a small council apartment (rented government accommodation), not the sort of place you would imagine someone would live in, considering the expense he was going to incur travelling to Singapore by car.

When Brian answered the door, I was even more surprised: He was average looking with very thick glasses and a stocky build. He was in his sixties, had grey curly hair, very bushy eyebrows and looked unshaven.

His place was unclean and pretty messy with all kinds of books, magazines and paintings scattered around. "Come in," he said, "Be careful of the paintings." Before he asked about me, he was telling me he was an artist, and that was how he made his living.

He mentioned that his eyesight was failing and that this was going to be his last big trip, one final fling while he could still enjoy it.

"I have wanted to do this for many years. Do you mind camping, as we will have to travel as inexpensively as we can?" I told him that was alright with me. Then he asked. "For such a long trip do you have a working knowledge of cars?" I assured him that I did. He went on and said that he would be more comfortable knowing that minor problems could be fixed on route. I told him that I would carry a number of tools to make small repairs if needed.

During the interview, Brian made me a cup of tea which was not very good. It would appear that from what I observed, his vision and coordination were quite impaired. Considering that, I couldn't imagine how he produced such beautiful paintings; at least that was my opinion.

One week later he called and asked me if I wanted the job? Without hesitation, I said that I did. We made arrangements to discuss the trip and when we would be leaving, plus all the things we would need for the long journey. The adventure was now a reality, and my mind was very focused on the trip. Between our meetings to finalize the details, I had to think about what to take.

5

I would not need much in the way of heavy clothes, as we would be in a warm climate the whole time.

I asked Mr. Turner about the applicants he had for the job. He told me that the list of people who had applied had been one hundred and twenty-six. He told me that he read every application. He had read some a few of times. His final list to interview became 26.

I would imagine it would have been quite the task to rule out the one hundred applicants that he had considered not suitable for the job. The applicants Brian said were a very interesting group, among them were ex-British policemen, a retired C I A (USA intelligence), a retired police investigator and others who wished to travel. There were some with no real skills, and a few too young to even consider. I asked him, "why me?" He answered, "My decision was based mainly on personality and psychology." In any case, we were both satisfied.

In his apartment again, the first thing on his agenda was a car. There were two cars his friend had offered him for us to take a look at; one British car and one American, the latter being a left-hand drive with an automatic transmission. We drove straight to the garage to see both cars side by side. The British car was an Austin Westminster which the most appealing of the two. It seemed a lot sturdier than the Ford.

The Ford Comet did not look very solid and I could not help but wonder if it would survive the long trip to Singapore. The Austin drove very well, but needed new brakes and tires. The Ford drove alright; however, I was not used to an automatic and left-hand drive, as European cars had right hand drive. The mileage was lower on the Ford than on the Austin. The Ford definitely needed a paint job, some new tires, brakes, a new muffler, a power steering unit and a new heavy-duty battery. This was my thinking because automatics use more power, and cannot roll down a hill and keep going, so in my opinion, I suggested that the better car was the Austin.

The drive back with Brian was quiet. All he would say was my fact-finding about the cars was excellent. At the apartment, he said, "We do not have a lot of time. We are leaving in a week and "there are no other cars for me to look at that are big enough to make the trip. You can go home now and we will talk in the morning. Tomorrow, come over at about nine thirty."

The next morning I was up early. I was very keen to know what his decision would be, after remembering his look when he saw the Ford. On arriving at Brian's, he surprised me by saying, "Let's go out to breakfast, my treat." We went to the nearby town of Woolston and sat down in a little café. It was a place I knew well and liked.

We ordered our meals, and then he said, "All that you wanted completed on the Ford has been achieved. So what do you think?" To myself I thought what a trip this was going to be, in a car that in my opinion would give us trouble. He had decided on price. This was not my idea of a good mechanical choice, but how could I challenge my new boss's selection, especially at this stage? So I answered, "Well that's great, what colour are you going to have it painted?"

"White top and red bottom, so it should help to keep us cool on the hot days ahead." He then went on to say that he had quite a time on the phone with his friend, trying to persuade him to find a power steering unit and a muffler. These items have to come from London, and I don't think he believed anyone would notice by just having a drive around the block. I have struck a deal with him, and provided he can get it ready in time for us we will take it." I assured him he had made a good decision. I thought to myself that I would much rather drive the Austin. This was a Wednesday, and the car was to be ready to be picked up the following Monday morning.

On Monday morning, we sat in his apartment, confident the car would arrive on time. That was when he told me there was going to be a third person coming along with us as a paying passenger. His name was Tony and he really wanted to make the trip. Brian said, "This fellow is a chef and could be useful helping with some of our meals."

We were going into town as soon as the car arrived, to purchase some sleeping bags, cooking utensils, a tent, some lidos (blow up air beds) and a tremendous amount of canned food. We had filled two shopping carts, and the weight was going to be of great concern to me. I was wondering if the car's suspension was okay, and how the engine ran under such a load. I also hoped the brakes would last. I considered all of these mechanical things. This was going to be one big challenge for me, but on the bright side, the long journey was sure going to be interesting.

CHAPTER 3

The car arrived from the shop at eleven am. It looked like it was in fairly good shape, albeit it had a poor paint job. The paint was merely a cover up job, and provided it didn't take too long to get to Singapore, the rust would hopefully not come through.

We drove the car to another friend of Brian's to get the car insurance for the trip, all in my name. The car title was also registered in my name. To my surprise, Brian went to just about every bank that I knew existed. Each time he left a bank we drove to another one, his confidence and the look of satisfaction increased on his face. This was very amusing. Brian was accumulating an enormous amount of cash, for the start of the journey.

The car seemed to run very well and I was getting accustomed to the left-hand drive and automatic transmission. Buying parts for the car was a concern, not only because of the cost, but where would we locate other parts for our trip.

That evening I started to work on my parts list for the car, knowing it might be difficult getting all the things I needed as we travelled. The most essential parts would be a muffler repair kit, a brake master cylinder repair kit, a brake slave cylinder kit, a set of points, spare set of plugs, booster cables, fuses, a radiator repair kit and a small amount of the essential fluids. This was vital and I hoped I could persuade Brian to get it all. To be confident of getting to our destination we would also need brake pads and shoes, due to the excessive weight and extreme heat conditions we would be encountering.

The problem with all of this was not so much the cost, as the weight.

The actual cost would be a concern for Brian, as his budget was very tight. I knew it would be a worry in my own mind, to keep a car running over such a long journey. Brian seemed to think I was being overly cautious in my demands for the car.

The passenger that Brian decided to take with us was another factor, since we only had a two door car. He had to climb into the back and with his backpack, making space another problem.

I could not understand why Brian wanted to take a paying passenger.

Later this proved to be to my benefit, because Brian was not a wonderful traveller. Tony and I became good friends and it was great to travel with him.

Tony was a chef, and later this proved to be a real bonus. He was to bring his own necessities, tent, sleeping bag, and cooking equipment, should he decide to go his own way at any time. I now had a real good travelling companion around my own age.

The shopping trip was an adventure, as I knew Brian was planning on buying non perishable goods so we would not have to do too much shopping en route. The amount Brian purchased was immense: We had two shopping carts, overloaded with practically ninety percent tinned food consisting of soups, pasta, vegetables, meats and fruits.

My mind was working overtime, trying to figure out where we were going to store all this material for an even weight distribution.

With this much weight in the trunk and a passenger with luggage, the painting equipment, and camping gear. I had visions of the car's suspension not lasting the journey.

Brian said, "Don't worry; we will re-organize them around the inside of the car. We will be fine as I have confidence in you, and I know you will make it safe." The car was only designed to take five people with their luggage, not huge amounts of canned food plus camping equipment, pots, pans, camp stoves, bedding, and tent. The plan now was to pack the car on Saturday, and leave on the Sunday morning ferry from Southampton. It was a trip I had made many times, but never with a car.

"You're on your way; be sure to lock the car up at night. That's our, food for the trip, we don't want to have to buy too much on the way, it's extremely expensive down there, and I need the funds for gas." Driving the car for the first time on my own was a real thrill; I could hit the gas and see how she performed. The three mile road home gave me a good chance to see how fast and smooth she would perform. There was not too much traffic, so when I could see it was clear, I floored it, and it kicked down so it picked up speed very well. I took it up to 75 mph. But I did not feel overly confident in such a big car, as all I had ever driven was a small four cylinder car with right-hand drive. Such a big vehicle would not fit on the drive between my parents' home and our neighbours', so I had to park it nearby at my grandmother's house.

After only two more nights at home, I would be off on the ferry to France and into a world of adventure! The most appealing thing to me was travelling to countries I had never been to before, and the warm weather. Packing was my next task; I had to get everything ready a day before so that we could have a trial run with all of our luggage and equipment. Tony had already said that all he would have was a rucksack.

I packed two small bags: one shoulder bag, and one small suitcase, not a lot when you considered that I could be gone for two to three months. I must have packed and repacked a dozen times, I considered the weather we would encounter. It would be warm or hot in the daytime and cool at night. I had one sweater, one light jacket, three short sleeve shirts, six t-shirts, 1 denim shirt (long sleeve), two pairs of shorts, one pair of jeans, two pairs of swimming trunks, four pairs of socks, four pairs of underpants, one pair of light shoes and one pair of running shoes. I expected we would wash our clothes frequently. There was also my journal, maps of Europe, small chess set and pack of playing cards. Tony had packed very compact, just his backpack. This was to allow him to leave us at any time, and stay at some place he might like. We were going to be on the move most days. We would not be staying anywhere very long. He was well set up with a light tent, sleeping bag, small stove and a set of cooking utensils. The entire pack with everything including, water and some food was only fifty-six pounds.

I was restricted, and could take only the bare essentials for the car; oil, a muffler repair kit, brake fluid and a radiator repair kit. It was scary to imagine what could happen in the heat and conditions we might encounter.

We were leaving home in a ten year old automatic, American car. It had sixty-four thousand miles on its' speedometer. I found it exciting, as I was starting a new chapter in my life.

As I was about to leave, my dad said to me, "Please come home safe and sound, son." Those words would always stay with me. There were no tears from my mother, just a pleasant smile as I drove away down the lane. They both stood on the road and waved as I disappeared from sight.

CHAPTER 4

The date to leave was now set for Sunday 20th June. We would leave by the car ferry from Southampton at eleven-twenty in the evening. I drove over to pick up Mr Turner, and then we were on to Woolston to cross the Itchen River on the floating bridge. (This is a floating platform pulling its self across the water on cables by an engine).

Our load plus this challenge of level loading would pose a problem, depending on the tide. If the tide were low going down, the ramp onto the ferry would be at a sharp angle. If it were upward, the slope to get on the floating bridge would be alright; however if the slope were downward, it could pose a problem. If the car was very low at the back end, due to the massive amount of food and camping equipment inside, it would be difficult to level out.

It was my worst nightmare, the channel tide was out and the slope down to the ramp was steep. We slowly approached and attempted to get on it carefully but this was to no avail. When the car dragged on the ramp, I asked Mr Turner to get out and walk.

He was not impressed and said "Why do I have to get out?" I explained that this may allow more clearance to get the car on the floating bridge with less weight. We have to get as much weight out of the car as possible, and I will try again at an angle that may be enough. He replied "Try on the angle with me in the car, as I do not want to walk". I backed up and tried again, inching along at an angle but it still hit the ground.

I told tell him to get out and I would try one more time. The only other alternative was to go around the peninsula to the Itchen Bridge. However that was a few miles north, and time was not on our side. We had no choice, since we had booked this ferry crossing of the Channel Brian quickly got out of the car, causing it to tilt at a very steep angle, I slowly dragged the car a little, so it levelled out and we made it on okay

When we parked on the floating bridge, I checked the car; I was concerned about the muffler and undercarriage clearance. There was no major damage, just a couple of scrapes. We were going to have the same problem getting off on the other side. Mr. Turner then walked back and sat in the car for the journey. I had a concern at customs since we had a massive amount of food and supplies plus all of Mr Turner's painting equipment in the car. When we reached the terminal, we had to look for Tony, our paying passenger. There are several entrances at the approach to the ferry. I knew this well, as I had been on the ferry many times to visit a friend in Paris. This would prove to be a great advantage, since a few of the people at customs already knew me, they would be less inquisitive and we would be cleared quicker.

As we approached the ferry check-in area, we were directed to the vehicle checking area. This was a new procedure, and I had no idea what to expect as I had always walked on and off. The custom officials asked us to get out of the car and show our tickets and passports. "Where are you going?" he asked.' Mr. Turner had already told me in advance to let him take care of any questions. Mr. Turner was extremely unpredictable; you never knew what he was thinking or might say. He told the official that we were going to Europe on a camping holiday and would be stopping at places that would suit him to do some scenic painting. Listening to him made me wonder why he made a statement like that, and why he did not mention our planned trip to Singapore.

Our paying passenger arrived, with his backpack in tow. This was the first time I met him. He was a short young man, with a beard, very slim build and medium length hair. Tony introduced himself. He was not like a person I imagined who would have applied for this job. I introduced myself and we waited for the conversation to finish with Mr Turner and the custom official. They asked me to open the trunk and I had to pull out the painting equipment in order for them to see all our food and supplies. At this point, I wondered if they where going to let us leave.

A voice from behind me yelled, "Where you going now with this lot, Alan?' It was one of the head customs officers. He knew me well. We were long time school friends and we often met for a drink when he was off-duty.

I had never brought back anything over the limit from my previous trips to Paris, but each time when I was asked if I had anything to declare, I would jokingly say, "Yes 10 bottles".

He would respond "yea sure, they must be miniatures in that small shoulder bag that you are carrying."

The grim look on Mr Turner's face changed to a smile when he saw our friendship. He said "Tell him where we are going, Alan, and that you are my driver," I proceeded to do so.

"This sounds like quite a job, you are the adventurous type, so I assume this will suit you, I guess you will have a lot to tell me next time we meet to have a drink," my friend joked. When all the checking was cleared up and finalized, I carefully re-packed all the food and camping equipment and our supplies in the trunk. Then away we went to get on the ferry. Once on board, we went to the restaurant, where to my surprise Mr Turner said to us "whatever you want to eat is on me. Make the most of it because once we are on the road, we will not be eating in fancy places!"

As Tony was the paying passenger, he had struck up a deal to pay for the gas, and help with the meals. I suggested that I would like to have a beer as I would not be drinking so much since I was the designated driver.

"No problem" said Mr. Turner.

For an overnight passage across the English Channel you can book a cabin or a recliner chair. Mr Turner had booked a cabin. Tony and I had recliners for the eight hour passage, I had never considered a cabin to be worthwhile, so Tony and I were in the cafeteria having breakfast at five in the morning; and then we met Brian on the car deck when we were ready to leave the ferry.

With all of us in the car, and Tony's backpack weighing about 55 pounds, I thought for sure the ferry would be lower in the water. Coming down the ramp off the ferry could pose a real problem. I mentioned my concern to Mr Turner, who now wanted to be called "Brian" from then on. He understood the situation better and had a change of attitude. He was now ready to listen to my concerns. I assumed he now realized I had his interests and safety at heart.

I saw a grin from Tony in the back seat. We had hit it off right away, and we would soon become very close friends.

When the ferry ramp came down, it looked pretty even, with not much of a slope. A crew member on the ship directed all the vehicles off the ferry, and you simply had to wait your turn. Brian was getting impatient and asked why it was taking so long. I told him to calm down.

They unloaded the ferry a certain way, as to keep it at an even weight. The ship was low in the water with the load it was carrying which would change the ramp level. I just hoped it was in our favour and levelled out. At that moment it was low, but it would rise, as soon as everything came off of the boat. We had a short wait, as there were just two cars ahead of us. The ramp looked perfect for our heavy load, and low riding car. As we exited the ramp we felt a very slight bump, but it was nothing to be too concerned about.

A customs officer was now directing us to another area to get checked out because our car was riding so low. This was not a great situation and Brian became very nervous. He asked, "Do you know any of the people working over here?

I said "Sorry I have only ever gotten off the ferry as a foot passenger; this is a new experience for me crossing over in a car."

We had to pull almost everything out of the car and the trunk. The custom officers who were looking at all the food and supplies remarked that we must be planning on an extremely long trip. They went through everything in great detail. They even asked us to open our bags, and Tony had to unpack his backpack. They wanted to know why Tony was carrying a backpack, unlike both

17

of us who had a suitcase each. They wanted to know why we had painting equipment. Even with Brian's easel, they still needed convincing that he was indeed an artist going on a trip through Europe. After almost an hour delay, we repacked the car, and headed onto the highway.

Our planned route was to head first through Northeast France and Germany. We then probably would go through Austria and the Alps, the Aegean and the Mediterranean areas, then Turkey, the Middle and Far East and onto to Singapore. At least these were the areas covered by maps we had. We hoped that English would be the universal or second language as we were not really fluent in any other tongue. In most of Europe this was the case.

CHAPTER 5

We drove south along a single lane roadway and down avenues of trees in France for what seemed like hours. It was a beautiful sunny day, not a cloud in the sky, not even a breeze to move the tops of the trees. We passed a few large cemeteries where World War One and Two victims were buried in rows with small white wooden crosses. Alsace-Lorraine was an area that for centuries had been highly contested by the French and German armies. I must mention our progress in my first postcard to my mother and father, which I will post later in the day.

We were driving through some very pretty villages and towns with occasional views of a rivers and canals. The views were what I would call extremely picturesque, and most certainly worthy of being painted. When I mentioned this to Brian, he commented that we would come to many more interesting places, especially when we reached the Rhine Valley in Germany. He was keen to travel as far as possible due to the long delay at the ferry customs dock.

The first day took us thirty-five miles south of Amiens to Beauvais, a town about 200 miles south of the English Channel. We encountered some very heavy road traffic, which made for a slow and very poor travelling day. I was the driver and Tony was our map reader, as Brian's eyesight was not good at reading fine print, especially on maps.

I noticed that we were consuming gas at an alarming rate. This was due to the heavy traffic, our frequent stopping and starting plus the car was heavily loaded. It was late afternoon on Sunday, when we come to a very nice campsite. It had been a hectic day and we were all tired. We hoped to travel with better progress the next day.

Brian went into the campsite office to pay for our overnight stay.

I had to set up the tent for Brian and I. Tony had his own tent and he pitched it next to ours. Brian sat on his shoulder bag, while Tony and I reclined on the bumper of the car to eat. Dinner that night was oxtail soup, crackers, and some tomatoes. The ground was not too even, so I had to jump up and down on the lumpy grass mounds to try and level it out so we could sleep better in our tents. Even with an air mattress it was not easy to make it level enough for Brian who could not get comfortable.

At one in the morning, there was lot of noise in the small village just across the field from where we were camping. Tony and I got up. Many people were out of their tents too, wondering what the commotion was. There was a dog barking and people yelling in French. Not being able to understand or speak much French, we asked around. We were told there was a dog with rabies on the loose, and they were trying to catch it. Then we heard a police car siren. Moments later, a shot was fired. We were told later that they had shot the dangerous dog as it had bitten someone.

Monday morning, we all got up late. We packed up after a light breakfast of cereal bars and juice. We left the campsite at eleven thirty, late considering the 300 mile distance we planned to travel each day. We were falling behind with our planned travel agenda. Brian had not shown any interest in painting anything. It seemed strange to us, we had driven past some very nice rivers. Much later on, we would know the reason why.

Heading for the town of Reims in the Champagne District, Brian decided to look for a coffee shop and stop. This was strange coming from him, as he wanted to get many miles in before dark. It was 2.30 in the afternoon when we finally stopped at a small roadside café.

It was a small but modern café, with four very neat round tables, white wallpaper with small white chairs. It was typically French; brightly lit and painted pink and gray, with, still art pictures on the wall.

The fresh, hot coffee that we yearned for proved to be a very welcome treat.

We met a young English student from Singapore, David. He was tall and thin, with short, blond hair and blue eyes. He had an extremely clear completion. He spoke with a distinctive English accent, which to me sounded like a Yorkshire accent. We were all ears. "Singapore, that's where we are headed," I said.

Brian said. "My driver is an experienced traveller and quite capable of taking care of almost any situation. What would you estimate our time to Singapore would be, Alan?

"Well assuming we pick up our daily travel rate, an average 500 miles a day, approximately six to eight weeks from now. The roads ahead would be an adventure, as unexpected things can happen.

I continued, "We can expect heat in Europe with sand storms and hot temperatures in the Middle East. The borders might be difficult to cross. We may not be able to take the direct route that we planned, and we would have to constantly make changes in our planned agenda."

We thought that Turkey was a fairly dangerous Asian country to travel, but still safer to go there rather than some other Asian country and only stopping overnight in certain safe places. I had read stories of trucks being hijacked in remote areas of Turkey. The English student was quick to respond, "You are wise to be realistic about this, even though I have not heard any news of car hijacking recently."

"Alan, I detect a strong Hampshire accent. Are you from South or North Hampshire? I would say Southampton, or any small town north of Winchester. "You're right David; my house is just a little east of Southampton. I would guess you are from Leeds." Correct, I am from Leeds."

"As for the hazards travelling in Turkey, when hijacking happens, cars and small vehicles are not the targets. The robbers are looking for goods for the Black Market. The haulage trucks in remote areas are their prey."

Tony suggested "We should get some newspapers and listen to any news on the radio. We are a long way from Turkey, and there have been no such hijacking problems for a while in that area," I replied.

He went on to say, "We should also talk to as many people as possible in the places we stop, and find out all we can about the countries ahead of us. There will be lots of people coming from that direction. Let's just hope we can find some who speak English."

We travelled on to the town of Metz, near the German and Luxemburg borders in the province of Alsace-Lorraine. This was an area that, for centuries had been highly contested by the French and German forces. Brian was anxious to get to a bank in town. The car was beginning to run unevenly. I got out, lifted the bonnet (hood), and discovered that the muffler was leaking. I could fix it but it would be temporary. We would need a new part; maybe we could get one in Metz near Verdun and Germany. I was aware of the conditions, we could expect by running a low and heavily loaded car; it would not hold up without a new muffler! I needed some thin, tin material, much like an empty pop or soda can. It's not something we had with us. We would have to drive on at a steady rate until we could get what we needed. I assured everyone it was only a small leak and we just had to drive slowly and it would be alright.

We set off again, with a considerable loss of power, pulling onto the main road and getting up to speed very slowly. When we reached 50mph we were fine. We were moving through some very nice countryside; open fields with cattle and some wheat or barley. About twenty miles later, we reached a small town with a garage. I pulled in and we filled up with gas and asked the worker if he had any old oil cans. He told us to take whatever we could use from his scrap pile at the station rear. We did. I explained that the muffler was too hot to fix right now, and that we would have to wait awhile and use these as a temporary fix.

Brian was impatient and wanted me to fix the car as quickly as possible. Mentioning there must be a bank in town, he went for a stroll to pass the time and do his business and some sightseeing.

I prepared what I needed, and pulled out all the things from the trunk or boot, since all the tools were at the bottom. Tony was helping me unpack and get my tools and repair kit. The man at the garage was intrigued by how many things we had in our car. Upon hearing me mention a bank, he said, "There are three banks in the town which are within a 10 minute walk from here."

Brian (who sometimes had a hearing problem) heard him and asked "Which way do I go and where are they? Are they close to each other?"

The mechanic replied, "No, one is on the main street; you will see it as soon as you walk down the main road. The others are on streets to the left and right, not far apart."

"Great, I will walk. Alan, you and Tony, do what you can when the car cools down. I will be back in an hour or so."

I found a large oil can and Tony took my tool and repair kit out of the trunk. The man from the garage spoke reasonable English, and asked, "How are you going to fix the leak with that can?"

"First, I will cut a strip out of the side of the can, at least enough to go around the muffler joint; then cut small slits from each end to form a double ended cone. I will then fill the leak area with this black putty. It will set very hard with the heat from the engine. That is why I have to wait for it cool down so I can make a mould around the manifold bracket. I have some pipe clips to pull the tin tightly around the putty mould to form a secure and leak proof job," I explained.

"Have you done this before?" the man inquired.

"Yes I have and it worked well. On one trip it took me 80 miles home and lasted for some time after that."

Tony and I then sat in the shade of the garage office. It was a very warm day, so waiting for the engine to cool down enough, would take a while. We waited about 20 minutes and then we cooled the manifold with some water. I then proceeded to make a neat, smooth shape using the messy black putty around the manifold joint. One can smooth this nicely with a little water. I wrapped around my tin shape, and placed two pipe clips on each side of the joint. It tightened up until the putty started to squeeze out slightly. When the putty set with the heat of the engine, the tin and clamps did their job. They were only there to keep it from moving when I started the engine. I had sealed the leak very well, but now we had to let the car idle up to temperature in order for the putty to harden.

An hour passed before the car was ready. Now we just had to wait for Brian to come back from town. Ten minutes later, Brian walked in saying, "Well guys, we do not need to stop at more banks today. How is the car?"

The garage man said, "Your driver has done a terrific job. It runs well."

"Great how long do you think it will last?" asked Brian.

"On a smooth highway I would reckon approximately 100 miles," he answered.

Brian said that we just had to get over the German border; then we would stop at the first camp site we come to.

"Are there any sites showing up on our map, Tony?" asked Brian".

"There are plenty showing up all along the Rhine River,"

CHAPTER 6

We crossed the German border without any trouble and looked for our first campsite. Arriving at one on the Rhine, a beautiful place, we camped with a view of the river. The river is the water highway in Germany and, a large amount of bulk freight travels this highway for cargo ships and long boats. We drove to the office of the first campsite we came to. It was only five minutes of driving along the river when we reached what looked to be a good spot.

Brian yelled "Drive over to the office Alan, and I will book us in for the night. You stay in the car Tony. I will take care of the fee for tonight". He did not mention how much he paid when he came back. He just told us to park and to pitch the tent not too far from the washroom.

I mentioned to Brian that it was beautiful spot to set up and do some painting. I received no immediate response. Then he said "There will be many more exotic and picturesque places. I want to get a lot farther into our journey before I can relax and think about settling somewhere to do some painting. True, this was a nice place, but it's probably been photographed and painted a thousand times. When I reach a place that is unique to me, I will paint it."

Tony was busy cooking our evening meal of peas, carrots, new potatoes, and ham. He did an excellent job when you consider he had only two small propane gas burners. The potatoes were cooked very well, and the carrots were tender, just the way I liked them. We had the peas cold right out of the can. It was a rough meal typical of camping, but when you are hungry everything tastes marvellous. We also enjoyed a loaf of bread that Brian had bought in town while we where fixing the muffler.

Tony and I agreed that Brian would never leave his shoulder bag unattended and kept it with him at all times like it was a part of him and never left it alone even taking it to the washroom with him. Tony and I started to think that he kept all his money in there since we noticed there was far too much money to fit in any wallet. We noticed it was full of UK pounds and French francs and soon also would hold German marks, just as soon as we found a bank first thing in the morning.

After we finished the meal, Brian asked, "Would you like to go for a cold beer somewhere."

"Most certainly" Tony and I replied.

Tony and I quickly packed up everything from our dining area on the grass. My job was the washing up in the nearby facilities, quite often with cold water. Returning with all the dishes and pots cleaned, Brian handed me some money and said "Take yourself and Tony for a drink. Don't wake me when you come back, enjoy, and remember, Alan you are driving tomorrow."

It did not worry me as a couple of beers were fine, but I would have a bite to eat later. "Thanks Brian, have a good night." I said.

Walking out of the campsite, it was only about four hundred meters and we were on the main street of the town. We decided to stop at the first tavern we found. We did not want to walk too far in the dark in a strange area. We entered to the music of a piano, accordion, and flute. A small trio was playing very nicely— not loud, but just enough to create a welcoming atmosphere. "Bonjour", the barmen said as we walked in, thinking we were French. As Tony has a beard, he must have looked more like a little Frenchman.

"Good evening" I replied.

"Great, my English is better than my French. What would you have?"

"I will have a small lager. What do you want Tony?"

"The same sounds good to me"

"Have a seat boys, I will bring it over"

It was a large bar and only half full; it seemed like a very charming place. Not knowing if any of the people could speak English, we just said "Good evening" as we passed by the musical trio moving towards a quiet table for two.

Small brass lamps lined the walls, along with some small, scenic oil paintings. There was a very large cornice in the corner of the ceiling, a chair rail, a very large baseboard, and small tiles on the floor; they looked like polished red brick. The furniture was all carved wood and looked antique, but in need of a coat of polish. It all had that well used look.

The barman brought our drinks, and I asked him how much. He smiled and said, "You can settle with me when you leave. Enjoy the beer and the music. You can just show me your empty glass if you want another."

"Thank you, sir"

"You're very welcome mate," he answered politely. The sound of the music in the background rose over the conversations in German. It was as if we were in a typical alpine bar, not a small town bar in a village.

"Tony what do you think of our adventure so far?"

"Not too eventful yet, I am not sure how far this car will take us, and Brian is always looking for bank. Why? We have not had great expenses yet. I would have thought he had enough funds to carry us through Europe and Asia now after going to so many banks."

"Good point. You've been paying for half the gas.

"That is true. Did you realize how happy he was when he came back to the garage in France? He obviously achieved what he wanted to at that bank. Look at how readily he told us to go for a beer and leave him alone. He gave us money for drinks. That was a sign of generosity that was not like him."

"You're right; I guess he wanted to be alone to count his money or his precious possessions in the shoulder bag."

Tony remarked. "We will have to be more aware of his mood changes from now on."

"Do you think you will continue with us to Singapore or leave us somewhere you might like to tour around? You have a backpack and can travel and stay anywhere at any time".

"Well, Tony, my plans are to somehow get to Singapore. I just hope the car will get us there."

"That is good news for me because I like you and we seem to get along well."

"I feel the same way. It's nice to meet someone like you, who likes to travel. I have always travelled alone because not many people are willing live out of a backpack." He then went on; "you seem to be very capable of solving any problems that come your way. I can understand why Brian chose you. Not many people I know would have been capable of fixing the car as well, and as fast, as you did".

"I appreciate the compliment, let's have another beer. We may not have too many more chances like this to relax. I remember on the ferry saying I would not have chance to have a beer, with all my driving. But I suppose that two beers would be okay. I would be able to sleep it off."

I knew, Brian did like to get up to early in morning. If we were a little late getting back, I may not wake up as early as I usually do. It would appear that the town had many late drinkers, even on Monday night as the bar was almost full. It was nice to see the barman had kept an eye on us, even though he was very busy. There was a very mixed group in the bar now, not many women, mostly men. It would seem like people who worked in the town, once finished work dropped in for a drink on there way home.

The barmen came over with our drinks again and asked if we were hungry. We had some light snacks and sandwiches." He returned with a large basket of chips almost like crackers, and a small bowl of what he called the bar's house meat and vegetable dip.

"Tony, you are the chef. Let me know what you think," I joked. He put a good amount on one of the crackers, ate it then took some more.

"Well what do you think, was it good?"

"If you want some, you had better start or I will finish it" he said with a big smirk on his face. Without saying another word, he grabbed a chip and dug in. It was excellent; a little spicy with a good tomato sauce. It proved to be a very nice snack to finish our beers with.

We really enjoyed this because our camp meals were nothing special. It was getting late, about 10:30. We had to leave soon. We needed a good night's sleep so we could be on our way early and get a fair amount of driving in.

The good part was we knew we were only about two hundred metres from our campsite. There are lights at the entrance so we would see it when we left the bar. We would use my flashlight to find our way quietly to our tents so as not to wake Brian.

The time has come for us to pay the bill and head back to our campsite. I walked up to the bar and waited for the barman; He was very busy, and seemed to be the only one serving at the moment. Immediately, he acknowledged my gestures and indicated that he would be over shortly.

When he dropped our bill on the table, he said, "No rush guys, whenever you are ready" Tony and I looked at the bill and decided to give him a nice tip. Leaving the cash on the table, we headed out of the bar. As we passed the barman, he thanked us and bid us a good night.

The road was well lit and we had no problem finding our way back to the campsite. The entrance had two small lights one on each side, and we needed our small flashlights to find the way to our tents. The grass was not short and with uneven ground we had to tread carefully. Our flashlights reflected off the car, so it was easy to find our way.

When I reached the tent, I got undressed rolled up my clothes, slowly unzipped the tent flap, and crept inside as quietly as possible. This was not an easy task since the tent was small and cramped. I settled down for the night. I fell immediately into a dreamless sleep.

CHAPTER 7

We woke at six, after a good nights' sleep. I snuck out and went for a shower. It was a warm morning; and the grass was damp. There was very little activity from any other campers. The washroom facilities were clean, but very basic. I turned the tap on to find there was no hot water. This was common in some inexpensive campsites. I did not mind the cold shower, but it was tough having a shave. I met Tony on the way back to the tent, and mentioned the cold water in the washroom.

He shrugged his shoulders and said, "Cold water is better than no water. You never know what you will get in these cheap campsites. I will make us some kind of breakfast when I return."

There was no sign of movement from Brian. He was still sound a sleep, so I sat in the car and completed my journal of the past events. Tony returned and we needed to decide what time we were going to wake Brian. Then, Brian moaned and groaned about how early it was, and what was for breakfast. Tony suggested cereal so we could get on the road quicker. "No problem, but can you make some coffee," shouted Brian. I got the cereal and Tony started boiling some water to make coffee.

Tony placed a table cloth on the trunk, a surprising luxury Brian wanted to have. He sat in the car to have his coffee and cereal, Tony and I just leaned on the car and had ours. When we were finished, Brian went to the washroom.

With his towel and shoulder bag over his shoulder, Brian stated "You can start packing up while I'm gone as we will leave as soon as I return." (His bag we now know contains more than just a few washroom items)

On his return, Brian was complaining about the lack of hot water. Tony packed quickly and all was neatly stowed in his backpack which fit right next to him on the back seat.

It was a bright sunny day. We were going to be very hot travelling in the car, with only the breeze from the open windows to keep us cool. We left the campsite heading for Munich. We were soon to be travelling on the German Autobahn which had no speed limit.

I assumed everybody would be passing us due to the fact we were really loaded down. I did not plan on travelling at a very high speed. When we reached the highway, I slowly increased my speed up to 70 mph. At this speed the car rode very steady. We were far from being the slowest, however many vehicles were passing us. Travelling at high speed in a heavy car was like riding waves in a boat, with a soft, almost floating sensation. We crossed many big viaducts and passed through some nice valleys, tunnels and forests. There wasn't much civilization out here, just a lot of traffic travelling along at high speed.

The highway journey was going fine, until I noticed the engine temperature was slowly climbing. This was the first time since we left the UK that I had been watching the temperature gauge and I became concerned. Earlier when the muffler blew, it had also gone up quickly. I was hoping my repair would hold up until we reached Munich in Bavaria. The time had come for us to get to a service station and check it out before it got worse. We would not want to break down or get stuck on the Autobahn as a tow out here would be very expensive.

As we approached a service area, I broke the news to Brian. I knew he would be very unhappy. His first reaction was for us to drive on a bit further, and slow down a little or to get off the highway altogether.

I told him that the British Austin Westminster would have been a better car I'm sure. But it was certainly too late to do anything about it now.

Like a good employee, I said "We should stop and try and find the problem before we go any farther." I explained that letting the car overheat could result in a blown engine and end the journey. I always had to explain to him the reason for stopping, since he always wanted to press on and get to the Orient as soon as possible.

I pulled into very large and fully-equipped, modern service station. We positioned ourselves, not far from the washrooms, at a quiet spot in the back parking area. I always had to keep away from the main busy areas when parking, if possible. This was a security request by Brian at the start of our trip, so whenever I could, I would comply with his wishes.

His main reason for this was not to draw attention to the many supplies we had in the car.

Brian immediately grabbed his shoulder bag and walked over to the service station. He returned with a pint can of coolant. This was not nearly enough to replace what we had lost from the engine in fluid, as we needed to increase the coolant to water ratio.

When the engine cooled a little I poured in the pint and it quickly disappeared into the radiator; not even close to filling it. Without hesitation, Brian headed back for more coolant. He then returned with sufficient to fill it. The repair was a complete success, so we got back on to the highway keeping a sharp eye on the temperature gauge.

A bright sunny day just added to the problem. The car would run hot, and so would Brian's patience and temperature. He hated stopping anywhere for too long.

The car could not shift into top gear, and this could cause it to overheat. We had to slow down and get off the highway again, as we could not proceed in second gear. Brian was now in a state of panic. We left the highway at the next exit and travelled along a regular two lane road looking for another garage. We were not far outside Munich where we hoped to get the muffler fixed. The transmission needed to be looked at so we could shift into top gear again.

We pulled into a filling station, to fill up and check the fluid in the transmission. This had to be checked with the engine idling. This was another thing Brian was not aware of about automatic transmission cars. After filling up we parked at the side of the station and lifted the car hood. The transmission fluid level was very low. This could pose a serious problem and halt our progress.

Brian bought a can of transmission fluid. We stopped the car, filled the container and ran the engine to check the level again. The level was now up to the line on the dip stick. As we eased out onto the road again, we had to hope that this was the only car problem. Slowly building up speed, the car shifted into second then smoothly into top gear. It would appear, we had resolved the transmission problem. With a big sigh of relief we headed on.

Tony was studying the map looking for an intersection to get back onto the highway to Munich, the home of Oktoberfest and beer halls.

He said, "The next exit is a long way from here. It may be quicker to go back and get on where we came off".

Brian was not happy about going back. "How far was it to Munich? What's the difference in time, as this road is quiet and looks good."

Tony answered. "If this road stays clear of traffic, we could be in Munich in less than an hour."

Brian said, "That settles it, Alan, we'll stay on this road."

He was quieter, probably thinking about his friend who had sold him the car. He was supposed to have serviced it well. From all the problems we have had, it really suggests that it was not serviced very extensively.

Brian asked me "should we look for another car in Munich, or fix this one at a garage?"

"Well you have to look consider, the options are fix or sell." I replied.

The problem was the transmission repair because parts could be very hard to find.

Brian was very quiet. It would appear I had given him a lot to think about. Time was his main problem. To stay in Germany would be very expensive. A few days for repairs would increase the cost dramatically.

There was no indication of what his budget for this journey was. As we were camping all the way, I would assume it was low.

"Alan "I agree with your thoughts on this, and we will have to assess the situation when we get to Munich. It may be wise to sell the car if possible. I will rely on your judgement as to what vehicle to get, so we may continue. A couple of days will not be too bad; however, we will need to find a campsite in or near the city to keep our costs down."

It was now late in the afternoon and Tony said, "We are not far from Munich and we should be able to make it there before dark. We should try and find a campsite as soon as we get there". "Tony studied the map for campsites near Munich. He had a map which showed camp sites but the ones with limited facilities did not show up. These we would find by asking people in the city. He found one nearby marked on the map, all we had to do was rely on Tony's directions to get us there.

CHAPTER 8

We arrived in a rural area, on a quiet road. Tony was not sure where we were, but we were winding along between valleys and hills with tall evergreen trees. We stopped again, with Tony, putting the map on the hood of the car tried to get our bearings.

Brian said "Tony, do you know where we are or are we lost?"

Upset by the delay, Brian grabbed the map and looked at it, holding it very close so he could read it. All he would say was we should be in a built up area and on a busy road by now. When he calmed down, we spread the map out on the hood of the car again and calmly traced our route and our destination. Locating our position on the map, it would appear that we missed a sign some miles back that would have taken us into Munich. (Munchen in German)

Now we had to go back. This was not a good idea as far as Brain was concerned. But it would be quicker. I explained that heading off route, into the countryside would be a gamble because the roads were small, and trying to find side roads to get back where we wanted to go would take too long. If we hit very rough roads, it would be a problem, as we would probably not have very much ground clearance under the heavily laden car.

While driving into the city, the transmission would not change into high gear again, and we were now in extremely heavy traffic with not too many places to stop. We made it into the city, and pulled into the first big garage, which was a Volkswagen dealership. I got out and walked over to the service bay. I asked if anyone spoke English, as I walked up to a mechanic, he pointed to the service manager's office in the corner. The gentleman spoke English well and was more than happy to have a look at our problem.

He said "Give me a few minutes and I will find a mechanic to assess your problem". Brian's first question was, "how much are you going to charge?"

"That is not a question I would ask at this stage, sir; let's see what the problem is and then we'll have an idea." You only have one other option and that is probably to be towed to another garage."

Very disgruntled, Brian mumbled, "well we had better let them take a look at it, and let us know if they can fix the problem and at what cost."

The service manager returned with a mechanic. "Let us take your car in and you can all wait in the customer service lounge, follow me."

Before we left it with the mechanic, we had to remind him it would only move around in low gear. It had a major transmission problem so a test drive would not be very successful".

"No problem sir, he we will just lift it up on a hoist and investigate."

The customer service lounge was comfortable; there was coffee, magazines and soft chairs. All the magazines and literature were in German, This was the national language and not one of us spoke it. Tony was content to read his book in English, while Brian and I had a coffee.

Half an hour later the service manager came in to inform us that the problem was not a big one, however the parts we needed would not be easy to locate and the time and labour costs would be expensive. The estimation would be approximately one hundred and fifty marks"

Brian had paid three hundred pounds for the car in England. With the value of the mark much higher than the pound, it would cost almost as much to fix as he paid for the car. Brian was totally stunned and sat quietly with his head in his hands for a few minutes. Looking up, he asked if it would take long to repair.

"We can fix it in about six hours if we can find the parts. I will have to phone around and see if I can locate them."

Brian replied, "We have no choice; we need to find a campsite."

"There is one not far from here. Our courtesy bus will take you there. We will help you transfer everything into the bus." With the help of the courtesy bus driver, it did not take long to clear the car and load the mini van.

"Now we have another problem, where will we store all the things we are taking out of the car? We only have one large tent and Tony's small one." I said.

Brian had already realized this, but was not concerned. He said, "We will worry about that when we get there."

The bus driver was amazed at how much we had packed into the trunk and surprised at the amount of tin food. As we headed for a campsite, Tony was studying the map to see where it was in relation to the garage. The driver and an older fellow and spoke very little English. All he did was point to his watch and say, "It's not far, it is ten minutes away."

Brian wanted to sit up front and I mentioned that it would be better for me or Tony to sit up front as we would need to see clearly where we were going. We should make notes and get a good idea of the route back to the garage. Without saying a word he gets into the back. The traffic got very light, and we were aware of the difference driving to the garage.

This was the first time travelling as a passenger for me since the start of our journey. Tony had our route on the map, he was good with the directions, but mentioned to me that I had better watch for landmarks and anything that would help us remember where we were. With all the turns he was making it would be hard to find our way back. We travelled along a main street for short distance and then down a narrow one-way street. The bus driver was familiar with the city and knows all the short cuts.

It was not so great going down one way streets in a city that was not familiar to us. That made for a very difficult return trip. The ten minute journey became fifteen minutes. We arrived at brick archway leading to a park by a river. We were at our campsite. The driver took us over to the registration office.

Brian went into the office with the driver and Tony. There were not many tents but quite a few camper vans, I noticed. The grass was cut short and the place was very neat and tidy. I could see a large washroom facility that looked new. This was nice but it probably would be expensive. It would be wonderful to have a nice hot shower in the mornings, I thought.

We all come out smiling and content, except for Brian who was a little apprehensive. He felt it was a problem being in one place for two days. It was not a good idea as far as he was concerned. He always wanted to camp and move daily, as his mind was always on time and money. He just wanted to get to Singapore as fast as possible with the least cost.

CHAPTER 9

It seemed very strange to have everything unloaded onto the grass
and have no car. Quite a few people were watching to see what
was coming off the mini bus. When I had finished pitching our
tent, Brian wanted everything put inside; but where were we
going to sleep. Brian explained to me that he had paid for two
tents, and we were going into the city to buy another one. Just
outside the campsite was a main shopping area and there were
quite a few large stores. We would be able to pick up another small
tent. He had asked Tony to pitch his tent with its opening opposite
ours and only a few feet away. His plan was to have another tent
pitched so that we have all of the tents with their openings facing
each other for security. Tony was happy to stay on the site and
look after everything until we returned.

I was walking out the gate beside Brian with his shoulder bag,
knowing now that it was full of money. I thought: this should
be interesting, Brian spending money, and us remaining here for
two days without a car.

Even though it was after 5.00 pm, there were still a lot of stores open, so we would have no problem finding a tent. We could see across the street a large department store. We walked across and went in. Brian walked very slowly, since he was not in great shape. I hoped that we would find what we wanted quickly.

In the store, I looked for any sign saying camping equipment, but all the signs were in German. Walking up to a counter, I motioned to a young girl, trying my best to explain what I was looking for. We were lucky she spoke English. She smiled and told us there was everything we needed downstairs at the back of the store. Brian looked around for the elevator. As soon as the shop girl realized he needed help, she came around from behind the counter and took us through the store to the elevator. When the elevator door opened downstairs, we were facing a large display of tents and camp supplies. The question being how much was he willing to spend. Walking around, I saw some very nice, full size, walk-in tents that looked great. The problem was not the size, but the weight, in the car. Brian bought a small ridge tent, simply for that reason.

"Well Alan", he stated", "The tent we have at the moment will be yours and I will sleep in this new one with all the supplies. We will be a lot more comfortable with this situation. All we need is to get the car fixed and get out of this city. Did you see any banks on the street when we came out of the campsite?"

"No, but I'm sure there are plenty in the city and they will be open in the morning."

"You are properly right, but we should ask the young girl upstairs who helped us".

When we approached the counter with our new tent, she was very quick to ask if we found everything we were looking for. I answered yes.

"We now need a bank. Are there any open and close by?" I asked"

"Not close by, but if you go out of the store and turn right, there should be one open until about 5:30. Get a bus or a cab and it will only take a few minutes."

Brian was glad that there was a bank still open. Outside, he told me to go back to the campsite and set up the tent and he would get a cab to the bank and see us later. I was very happy to walk back, knowing I would have my own tent to sleep in.

When I arrived back at the site, it was getting late and the light was failing. It would soon be dark. Tony helped me set up the new tent and we moved all the supplies into it before Brian returned. The new tent was nice and the extra space was perfect for our supplies. Tony was not surprised to hear that Brian had gone to a bank. He mentioned that we can be sure if there were more banks open he would have gone to all of them. It was now getting dark and there was still no sign of Brian, so we had supper and cleared everything away.

With a small portable light hanging from the top of the tent, we started to play a game of chess. Tony was my teacher and I learned as we played, only to lose every time. Then we played Cribbage, which we were more compatible at and it was more interesting for both of us. Then we heard Brian returning.

"How are you Brian, I asked, did you get to a bank?"

"Sure did", he replied. I had some supper in the same area. I hope you had supper. You have done a nice job putting up the new tent. Are all the supplies in it with room for me to sleep?" "There is plenty of room for you. It will be very comfortable, as you can now stand up inside".

Brian suggested we go have a beer, and he would look after things.

The most important thing to realize was that we were not moving in the morning and there were no time constraints.

The street was full of shops and well lit, so we would not have a problem finding somewhere to have a beer. After fifteen minutes of walking, we saw a really narrow street with a tavern sign. As we headed down the road, we came to a bar that had a very fancy crest of arms hanging over the entrance. It was quiet, but well lit.

I said to Tony, "Do you think should we try this?" There are more pubs in the distance. "We should go in as we have no idea what time they close". This was a week day and it was getting late. Walking in, we found a small comfortable spot to sit in the bar area, as all the tables were taken. It did not appear to have an English atmosphere. There was a dart board in the corner with two fellows playing a game. The barman came over to us. "gutteintaggen." (Which I think means good evening in German). I responded with "good evening, sir."

"You are very welcome and my English is fair because I married an English girl I met in London when we studied there." I would never have thought our luck would be that good two nights in a row.

I explained to him that last night, we were in a tavern on the Rhine, and the barmen there spoke English also. "I'm not too surprised as a lot of us over here went to university in England," he replied.

"No draught bitters here, so what would you like to drink boys?" "We will have a couple of lagers. "No problem he says" "we have Harp or Carlsberg on tap." "Great, I will have a Carlsberg, what you going to have Tony?"

"The same is fine for me". A nice barman always makes for a pleasant evening. It was late and the beer was good. Our server had time to talk to us since it was not too busy. "Where are you heading?" the barman asked. "We are going to Singapore" "That will be quite a journey, are you driving?" "Yes", I replied. "Wow that is quite some task to take on, just the two of you?"

"I am driving for an artist and Tony here is our paying passenger".

"I have had people in here who are touring Europe and often going down to Italy or Greece, but never anyone driving to Singapore. How long do you expect it to take to get there?" "There is no set time, but we assume six weeks."

"We are here at present because our car is being repaired. We have a transmission problem. The car is in a Volkswagen garage not far form here. We are in a campsite about fifteen minutes walk from here."

The barmen stated". "Those garages I know well, but they would be expensive, what type of car are you driving?"

"A 1966 Ford Comet two door coupe; it's an American car".

"They may be able to fix it, but getting parts could be a problem".

"I do know a few good repair options for you", he stated. "One mechanic is in the bar right now, would you like me to talk to him for you".

"The problem is the fellow I am driving for would have to be consulted, should we want to use another repair garage".

"Alright, I will explain your dilemma and ask if he could help you in any way".

The barman gave us our drinks then went over to an older gentleman with a small beard wearing an alpine hat. He spoke with him for a few minutes and the fellow nods to me with everything he tells him. When he came back, he told us the man would fix it with no problem, so he said, "If the dealership garages are unable to fix it for any reason, he would be happy to fix it and he would not over charge. He has a good workshop and is able to manufacture parts, since he was also a tool maker with some milling machines in his workshop. He has also rebuilt many old cars, and this would be a very interesting project, he would be pleased to take on the challenge".

"That is great, but how we can contact him?"

"He will be here at lunch tomorrow. This is his local pub and he is in a lot". His workshop is just across the road, left and about 3 minutes from here. It's on your right hand side, and you will see Herman's auto"

"Well Tony do you think, Brian will agree to move the car to repair it?"

"Herman will fix it at a lower cost." The barman asked him, if he could fix it tomorrow. He agreed. "Tell him it will be cash, with no bill required. I will bring the car to him late in the morning".

The barmen shouted something to the mechanic and he smiled and nodded his approval. The magic word to him was cash. "He will stop what he is working on and fix your problem right away."

'We will have to speak with Brian in the morning and get back to you at lunch time tomorrow".

Walking back from the washroom on the campgrounds that evening, I was greeted by Brian. He said, "Tony has told me that you have found an alternative repair man. That would be great, see if you can remove the car from the garage and get it over to him today, we will pay them for their efforts and take the car to Herman".

"Tony should remain here and you and I will grab a cab and go to the garage to move the car. 'Alright, what time will you get up? "You and Tony have breakfast when you get up and I will have something to eat on route".

Brian was not an early riser like us as we well knew. His mood was mind boggling. I wonder how many banks he got to today. He would have probably acquired as much cash as possible, knowing that the car repair was going to be costly. Now he can save money on the repair and maybe move out of Munich sooner.

On walking to the washroom the next morning, I saw there was a long line up. There was some kind of a problem. It would appear there was no power, and there was no hot water. The repair man soon came and after fixing it, he gestured to us to go on in and enjoy the rest of the day. I guessed that was what he said in German. I did not understand, but everyone walked in. This was one of the best washrooms I had ever been into on a campsite. There were two rows of six sinks with a nice big mirror along the wall above each sink. There was a stone floor, with white-tiled walls and strip lights over the mirrors. This camp ground was very big and held a large number of tents and camper vans. There were a few trees around the washrooms which is in the middle of the well laid out and scenic site.

Before I finished shaving, Tony walked in and said, "There is still no noise or movement from Brian. He must still be sleeping."

"Have you any idea what we will have breakfast, Tony?"

"Well" he replied, "We have some bread, peanut butter, fried onions and egg."

"Great, I will start frying onions if I get back before you".

"After a quick shower I will return and cook. We should wait and see what we will do when Brian rises, since one of the stoves is in his tent. I only have one and we could do with two gas stoves; one for eggs and one for the onions. There would be no rush and we could have breakfast together."

Tony got back to the tents before me and started to set up for breakfast, but the table and one chair were in Brian's tent. These were some items Brian bought from someone on the campsite I have one chair and I wondered why Brian did not leave the table, chair and stove in my tent so we could set up for breakfast. Waiting for Brian to get up, we sat in my tent and started to play cribbage.

Finally at eight-thirty, Brian stirred and came out, asking what was for breakfast. We told him what we had planned. He agreed with our eggs and onion deal. He said "I will go to the washroom, and you guys can cook breakfast. Get what ever you need out of my tent. There may be a can of spuds in there. If you cut them up, you can make some fried potatoes. We are going to have a really good breakfast, let's have all three stoves going, Tony."

Without any hesitation, I got the table and Brian's chair. I took two boxes of tin food out and put one on top of the other; and we had a third seat for Tony. "Well Alan, I need approximately twenty minutes to have everything ready, and that's about how long Brian is going to be."

Brian slowly walked over to the washroom with his towel over one shoulder and his brown shoulder bag over the other. We had cold drinks for breakfast, orange juice or water. I walked over to the main street to get some coffee. I was sure there would be a coffee shop open, as it was a busy street with people heading for their daily work in this lovely Bavarian city.

Walking over to the camp entrance, I wondered where I would find coffee.

I did not worry because as soon as I reached the street, there were lots of people walking by with coffee. I asked a few people, but I didn't get an answer. A kindly old gentleman asked "Looking for coffee, sir."

"Thank you, yes, where will I get some?"

He asked me to come with him and he would show me since he had plenty of time,

"How far is it? I have to get back to the campsite where my buddy is making breakfast"

"It's just two minutes away", he replied.

The shop was like a small bakery. It seemed like waffles were a favourite here, since everyone had waffles and coffee. There was a long shelf along the side with bar stools and I was very tempted to stay and have something. I picked up our two coffees and a tea. I remembered Brian liked fresh tea, not coffee in the morning. Thanking the gentleman who had escorted me there, I rushed back to the campsite.

I arrived back at the campsite with perfect timing as Tony was dishing up a hot breakfast. The hot drinks I brought were the finishing touch to a perfect start to the day.

All we needed now was some luck with the car, and I hoped we could get it to Herman's Auto. After washing up and walking back to the tents in the now bright sunshine, I noticed Brian was heading for the camp office.

I asked Tony where he was going, and he said the man from the office came over and asked about the extra tent. Payment in campsites was per tent, it seemed. Brian had to pay for the extra tent. He wanted to haggle for a lower price. Haggling was an old European custom.

"I assumed he paid a little more, but not full price. I'm sure with his cash; it would not be a problem to get a good deal."

Brian walked back, quite content, saying. "He gave us a good break". Since this campsite was very secure, day and night, Brian was now confident that we could all leave the site without any concerns.

CHAPTER 10

The main street in Munich was busy, but it only took a few minutes to hail a cab. The driver who spoke English had no problem getting us to the garage. On arrival at the garage, Brain gave me 40 marks in small bills and said. "Talk to the gentleman and pay him what ever is fair to get the car out for us"

Returning to Brian I told him, "The service manager was great and only charged us 20 marks", He said "I knew you wanted to get on with your journey, so the big delay wasn't good for you." Brian was happy as we proceeded to Herman's with the car.

Driving out on to the street in the direction we came in the cab, we hoped to trace the route back. The traffic was still a little heavy. This was convenient because the car was not shifting well so I could not travel very fast. We sped up a little in the traffic and to my surprise the transmission shifted.

"Great it seems good", said Brian", "But its cold and that may be the reason, I'm not confident. I do not assume it will work well when the motor warms up".

Tony seemed to think we were heading in the right direction, as the scenery was familiar. Fifteen minutes of driving and we were totally lost and not in the right area. Brian was getting frustrated, "Where the Hell are we? "I thought you guys could get us to Herman's auto.

Brian suggested that he would get a cab and we would follow him, as he figured a cab driver would know the way to the campsite and from there we could easily get to Herman's.

"Great idea, Brian let me pull over and try and flag down a cab for you".

Tony got out and haled a taxi. The cab stopped behind us and Brian got in. It took quite a few minutes of driving before the cab driver realized that we needed to follow him. We tried to stay behind him so we did not lose our guide. This wasn't easy, when you are driving on narrow streets with lots of traffic. I neglected to tell the cab driver that we had a problem with the car. The taxi driver was changing lanes all the way and I was sure he had forgotten that he was supposed to keep me in sight behind him. Then what I feared would happen, happened, he was in the right lane ahead of us and turned very quickly down a side street.

"We have now lost him and Brian", Tony said. "Alan, pull over and I we will check the map or ask someone if they know where the campsite is. We can't be too far away. Based on the map, we are very close. But with all these one way streets, it's hard to know how to get over there. Take the next right off this street if you can, then the next right and that should put us on the main street leading to the campsite."

We moved on very slowly. By now we were sure Brian was going crazy as he could not see us. He was probably upset with the taxi driver. We just hoped he got back to the campsite and was waiting for us. The directions Tony gave me were good and the street seemed familiar.

I heard a siren and saw flashing lights behinds me; it was a police car. This was a first for us. We had not encountered police before. I hoped they spoke English as I stopped. They pulled around in front of us. I hoped they saw my small union jack on the trunk. They both got out and walked up, one on each side of the car. The windows were open as we did not have air conditioning, so we could talk.

"Hello Sir", said the officer on the passenger side to Tony.

We are once again in luck, one speaks English. Tony was quick to say, "Good morning, how are you, sir?

"We noticed how slow you were travelling, what seems to be your problem?"

I explained about our transmission and that we were heading for a garage called Herman's auto. The officer on my side said, "Herman, I know him well. He is not very far down the street, we will escort you to him, follow us".

Then the one on Tony's side said "If he cannot fix it nobody can, he is one of the best mechanics we know. How did you become aware of him?"

I replied, "We were in a bar on the street right where his garage was located and the barman introduced him to us".

"Ok. Stay right behind us and we will escort you to his garage. It's about two kilometres away". As soon as we travelled down the street, we approached the entrance to our campgrounds and saw our site.

Brian stood on the street looking for us and when he saw the police car escorting us, he quickly disappeared into the campsite out of view. It was not hard to see a police patrol car with all its flashing lights. Brian was always nervous when the police were anywhere near him. Tony and I were curious about his reaction and later the reason why will become known.

Turning down the street past the bar, and our site, we stopped right outside the garage. We were attracting attention. Everybody was curious about why an American car was being escorted by the police. The garage door was open and Herman came out immediately. Both officers shook hands with him and pointed to our car and smiled. We got out of the car and handed Herman the keys. He thanked them and said something in German to the officers.

One officer turned to us and said. "Come back in two hours. He will know more and have an idea on the time it will take to repair. You have no need to worry, we are very confident he will fix it."

On arrival at the campsite, we explained the situation to Brian. He was satisfied with the recommendations that Herman would repair the car well and we would be on our way shortly. Then he asked, "Did he say when our car will be ready?"

"We will know in a couple of hours. I said. "The officers told us he would fix it; he was one of the best at fixing anything. "He loves a challenge and will make the part if he can not find it".

"When you come back from Herman's, I will take us all out to lunch, my treat. It's been a stressful day so far, we need to relax and enjoy the rest of the time here."

Just after midday, Tony and I headed back to the garage. As we were walking down the street we were becoming very familiar with the area. I mentioned to Tony that I hoped we could have the car fixed and move out of here soon. I was not sure how we were going to understand what Herman would tell us. How much and how long was the main thing we needed to know. The street to the garage was busy; there were lots of people and no cars. This must be a popular shopping area or a short cut to the main street.

We approached the garage and saw our car up on the hoist. Herman saw us and waved to us to come in. The transmission was neatly laid out in many pieces on the bench. He knew we did not speak German, so he showed us the best way he could, how it worked. He showed us a bearing and a small shaft that was badly worn. This was the problem. He pointed to the bearing saying "I buy and the shaft I will make". He would complete all the repairs for 100 marks cash.

We would tell Brian that the car would be ready late in the afternoon of the next day. The price was right, 100 Deutche marks. I thought this was a fair price.

Then we will leave for Austria the next day. "Do you think that's a good idea, Tony?" "Sure, provided Brian will not want to go to the garage, and he lets us take care of the bill."

"No problem, we just have to tell him there are always police in the area." He will give us cash as he does not want to go anywhere near them."

We explained everything to Brian without a problem. Then we went out with him for our lunch treat. As soon as we were out the gate, Brian walked in the direction opposite to the garage and hailed a cab. He told the cab driver to go to an address which he had written on a piece of paper.

After a ten minute cab ride we were outside a restaurant on the edge of a park. Brian paid for the cab ride and said "Come with me, there is a patio at the back of the restaurant."

The place was full, but there were more tables on the patio. The waiter pointed us to the back where the patio doors were. It was not an expensive restaurant; however it was very clean, bright and well decorated with countryside scenes and murals on the walls. Brian was not sure of the place and he looked behind to the door in a fairly obvious manner as we walked through.

As we were waiting for our server to bring the menus, I asked, "What are you craving, guys?"

Brian said, "You can have anything you want from the menu, and you can have a beer if you would like, Alan, you will not be driving for a couple of days, at least not until our car is fixed."

The waiter came over to us. He did not speak fluent English, but knew a few words. He handed us the menu. It was all in English and German. I decided on the veal sandwich with a Caesar salad. It was very reasonable. Tony ordered pasta and garlic bread and Brian, a steak. Tony and I asked for a Stella Artois lager and

Brian ordered his usual, a tea. Now we could just relax and enjoy ourselves.

"How did you find out about this restaurant, Brian?" "It seems like quite a nice place and I noticed you had the address written down".

"I was speaking to the man at the campsite office and asking about a moderately priced restaurant where we could go and have a nice lunch. This is the place he recommended". The service was wonderful, and the waiter was back quickly with our drinks. I had a feeling the food would be excellent.

We enjoyed a cold Stella on the patio next to the park. There were some big trees close to the patio which gave us a sufficient amount of shade from the hot sun. The patio was surrounded by a black wrought iron fence. We could actually use a few more days like this to relax and enjoy the scenery; however, I guess we'll have to see how things go.

It was nice to see him being generous for a change. We have to enjoy this. When we are back on the road soon, this kind of luxury will not be on the agenda, I am sure. The waiter arrived with our order which contained a great selection of dishes. Everything looked really good; I was really impressed. My veal sandwich and Caesar salad tasted great. The pasta plate for Tony, and Brian's steak looked very appealing. Had I known how good the steak looked, I might have ordered it.

The problem in Continental Europe is you can't be confident of meat being tender, unless you are in an expensive steak house. We all had a good lunch. We enjoyed another beer each; Brian was content drinking more tea.

He stated, "This was a thank you meal for saving me extra expense on the car. You both did well getting it out of that expensive garage. This was the least I could do for you, doing such fine job with the car." Brian decided on a dessert and motioned for the waiter to come over.

"Do you men want anything else to eat?"

"No, we are fine thanks". Brian ordered an apple strudel and ice cream and then he asked for our bill

It was now late in the afternoon and he was anxious to go back and check on the car. Brian pulled out his cash and asked what kind of tip he should leave the waiter. Tony and I both agreed that the service was excellent.

"How was your steak Brian?" "Very nice", he replied. "Then I would suggest fifteen percent of the bill is reasonable." Brian put the cash on the table.

CHAPTER 11

Outside of the restaurant, we hailed a cab for Brian to go back to the site. Tony and I decided to walk back and enjoy the scenery. Since we had not brought a map with us, we did not have any idea where we were. We came to a very narrow passageway for pedestrians only with small shops and buildings; we then came across an old tool store. Looking in the window, we realized it was extremely old. There were tools of every kind there: hand drills, chisels, screwdrivers, and all models of old planes. There was every kind of old tool you could ever imagine. This was a great place to look around. We felt that we were in heaven. It was not realistic to think of sending any home as it would be expensive. As we walked in, we could see it was narrow and went a long way back. All the shelves, from floor to ceiling were crammed with ever kind tool imaginable plus storage jars, jugs, earthenware, steel pots, clay pots, iron cooking skillets, and many old cooking utensils.

The owner of this store did not speak English. This was a good thing, because lacking money, we could not buy anything. So we kept saying "no money, no money", but she did not understand. All she was looking for was to sell something to "these rich tourists." This was quite a fascinating place for a tradesperson, like me. I keep telling her "nine, dachshund" (my attempt at speaking German) as we had to leave.

We were now back on the narrow street which we hoped would bring us somewhere near the campsite or at least be familiar to us. We would have liked to go into more of these stores and explore, as we were fascinated by what they had.

After walking for five minutes along the street, traffic became heavy but it was moving well on what looked like a main intersection. We were hoping to see something familiar, so we might know where we were. As we reached the next street, we recognized the area.

After five minutes, we could see our street leading to the camp grounds. We crossed over to the other side of the street but it was not too easy, due to all the traffic. At last, walking in the right direction, we felt confident that we were heading for the campsite. As we approached a small street on the left, we discovered it was the street where our car was being repaired. We decided to checkout the progress with the car as we had plenty of time. Herman said he was busy and we should come back tomorrow to check it out.

We went back to the bar, where the bartender, recognizing us, says. "Hello, would you boys like a cold beer-perhaps a Pilsner?"

We reply, "Sure, but give us a Stella each". We were going to enjoy this as we became very thirsty after our long walk in the heat of the day. You know what they say about Englishmen in the midday sun.

The barmen comments that he saw Herman at lunch time and he was progressing well with the "American tank" as he calls it. He tells us "Herman loves a challenge and nothing beats him. He finds a way to fix almost anything mechanical. When do you assume you will reach Singapore?"

"There was no set date, but six weeks was our best estimate. Due to car repairs and other delays, it's very difficult to judge. Brian, the elderly fellow I'm driving for, would like to get there as quickly as possible by driving at a reasonable amount everyday".

We told the barman that we must head back to the campsite now and will hopefully be in for a final beer and say goodbye tomorrow night before we leave. We thanked him told him we hoped he would have a great evening.

As we walked back Tony said, "I wonder if Brian will still feel generous and want to take us out to dinner.

"I'm pretty sure he will want to save money and cook tonight on site."

CHAPTER 12

It was late afternoon and Brian had been alone for a quite awhile. He would have had time to think about the plans for moving out as soon as we could. When we reached the entrance to the camp site, we couldn't see our tents. There were many more tents and plenty of camper vans on site now. The campsite was almost filled to capacity. We were lucky to have gotten a prime place right by the river.

As we approached our site, we saw Brian talking to an older couple. "Hi guys" he said; "This is Ted and Jean from London. They are retired and touring Europe, just like us." Brian then told us they may be travelling with us for a while.

"Ted and Jean have a big Ford campervan with a large pull out awning, right over there." He pointed towards the washrooms, where it was easy to spot the van with its big orange and yellow stripped awning hanging out on one side.

"It's very nice to meet you both, said Ted, we have heard all about your planned trip to Singapore. I met Brain coming back from the washroom. He had fallen outside and I helped him up. We then went to our van and had a drink. We are leaving in the morning and heading for Austria. When I told Brian, he said "you are heading there too".

"We have a problem with the car and it will be fixed tomorrow so we will leave the following day."

Ted was tall and of medium build with gray hair combed neatly back He has a moustache just like a military sergeant-major. He looked fit and very capable of helping Brian up. His wife Jean was pretty, with curly gray hair, brown eyes and a honey complexion. She did not look like she was old enough to be retired. She has a great figure and knew what clothes to wear to compliment it.

"We will leave you now to have your supper and Brian will come over later and play cards with us, while you two men go for your evening beer."

Tony and I looked at each other, smiled and said, 'that sounds good!'"

Brian's good mood continued; it was not something we expected. We had soup and crackers for dinner. After we were finished eating, we cleaned up quickly. Brian went to Ted and Jean's van to play cards. Tony and I went to town for a beer and to see the barman, who surely would be surprised, as he did not expect to see us again. As you can tell Tony and I enjoyed pubs.

Brian waved and shouted to us just before he entered the van, "Enjoy yourselves boys, I'll see you in the morning".

CHAPTER 13

As we walked towards the gate, Tony suggested that we head in the other direction and find a different bar. A young man approached us and asked us something in German. "We said "sorry we do not speak German."

He smiled and said, "Great you are English too. I'm learning German and I was looking for a bar somewhere for a drink. My name is Jan, and I am a university student."

Tony and I introduced ourselves to him.

"I live in a student residence down the street, and have only been in Munich two days, so I am not familiar with this area. Most of my associates have gone with some local chaps to a noisy disco, but that is of no interest to me."

"We are from a campsite on the main street about 15 minutes from here. I suggest you walk with us and go to this very quiet bar we know. It is on a narrow street with very old buildings and little shops. "That sounds like a very nice place, how did you find it?"

"We walked out of the campground one night, and came across this narrow street. As we strolled down the road and found the bar."

"This will be the first time we have come this way at night. I should tell you it's about a half hours walk from here." Jan was not concerned and was happy to have the company of fellow countrymen in a strange city.

"We could get a cab and split the fare what do you think?"

"I'm happy to walk, how about you, Tony?

"Fine, if we pick up the pace a bit, we will be there in less than twenty minutes."

We were soon at the entrance of our campsite which was less than fifteen minutes from the pub. When we reached the small street heading for the bar, Jan told us that this was an older area of the city which happened to be protected by preservation (heritage) orders.

When we all walked into the bar the owner greeted us saying, "I see that you fellows enjoy it here, I'm flattered!"

This was a fairly quiet bar, and exactly what the student was looking for. Jan was impressed. He started talking to the barmen in German. He returned and told us he intended to stay with us and have a few drinks. He wanted to practice his English with the patrons and did not want to walk back alone in the dark.

Jan was very keen to know more about our journey. We explained that the gentleman sitting opposite to us was fixing our car. We glanced at him and he acknowledged us by raising his glass.

The pub owner saw Herman every day, and he told us that the car would be ready by late tomorrow afternoon. Jan walked over and spoke with the mechanic. He returned and said that it would be a good idea for us to sit with Herman as he could translate.

We would know exactly what went wrong with the car. The mechanic was glad to explain all his work to Jan in German. The translation from Jan was not great, but I could understand that Herman had to manufacture a shaft and purchase the bearings, and then he would be rebuilding the gearbox. Jan was really helpful and I appreciated it.

It was getting late and Jan had to leave because he has a class in the morning. Tony and I suggested that we walk him back to his residence. It would be no trouble for us since we did not have to get up early in the morning. This would save him cab fare. Jan happily accepted our offer.

We said good night to the mechanic, and asked Jan to tell him in German, that we would come for our car tomorrow after lunch.

Herman replied, "Tell your friends to come at about 3.00 pm, it will be ready by then." We shook his hand and said good night.

We walked out to the street. It was very dark and the street lights were dim but adequate enough to see the narrow side walk. The street was quiet as not too many people were out walking. There was also hardly any traffic. We walked at a good pace, and soon reached the intersection where we met Jan. He was fine to walk from there to his residence. He thanked us for a very nice evening and said he was glad to meet such fine gentlemen, who insisted on escorting him home" He wished us a safe and trouble-free journey to Singapore.

The evening was long, and having walked a few miles, we knew we would sleep well and not be up early.

CHAPTER 14

The next morning I woke up to the sun shining brightly on my tent and Brian talking outside. "Good morning boys, how is everyone this fine morning?'

We told him we had a good nights' sleep and felt well rested. He continued, "I have made coffee would you like some?"

It was now nine o'clock, and we decided to take a walk down the main street.

"Tony, do you think we should look in on Herman to see how he's doing with the car or should we come back at 3:30?"

"No, don't bother him. We should enjoy this morning at the museum while we're here."

As we passed the garage we could see the car on the hoist and the gear box in pieces on the bench. It was about ten o'clock. When we reached the end of the street, we crossed over and there was a sign directing us to the museum. We saw from the map, it was a long way past the restaurant and had a nice park at the back.

We could see a large old building. It looked like a church without a steeple. It was an old and impressive structure.

This was their national museum of art. We were extremely interested and went in. The building was very quiet, and there seemed to be more security than visitors. The place had three floors and was larger than it looked from the outside. The next 2 floors were the most interesting with very old tools and implements used for cooking. It was mid-afternoon, about 2.30 pm, and we were a thirty minute walk from the garage. We would soon have to leave. About three o'clock, we headed for the garage.

We reached the garage right on 3.30 pm. The car was now off the hoist. We went in and looked for Herman. We heard a banging of glass and saw Herman in the far corner a small office. He beckoned us over and showed us some small parts. His English was good enough for us to understand him. He smiled and looked very pleased with himself.

I gave him 100 marks cash; he gave me the keys and said "you try the car out and come back to let me know how it rides. "We were very surprised he knew so much English, even if it was basic. We got into our car and drove out. I was anxious to see how well the gears shifted.

The maps were in the car's glove compartment, and Tony directed me out of the garage onto the main street. Soon we left the Volkswagen garage and headed for the highway. The car was now running well and shifting gears perfectly. I hit the gas on the highway and we went very quickly, shifting smoothly at high speeds. We headed back, knowing that Brian would be happy, because it was running smoother now than it ever has since he bought it.

CHAPTER 15

We drove back in the heavy traffic without any problems. As we approached our campsite and drove in, we realized we couldn't drive over to our tents because there was no clear route. There was a large van obstructing the way, so we parked by the office.

Brian went into the office. He was not very long and came out a little unhappy with the situation. He said "the people who own the van will not be back until late tonight, so we need to move our car." The campground owner will help us move our supplies to our car with a large dolly. The gentleman came from the back of the office with a great four wheeled dolly with a steel pull handle. It looked capable of moving all of our supplies in one go.

Tony and I told him that we would load it. Brian came over and said, "Take everything to the car that we will not need tonight. We will keep the dolly for the night and take the rest of our gear over to the car when we leave in the morning."

The dolly was a good size so we could shift what we did not need for the evening. We started loading the boxes. Brian announced he was going to ask Ted and Jean if they would help. To our pleasant surprise, Ted and Jean returned with him. We loaded everything on the dolly. With Tony and I pulling and the others pushing, it was easy to place the heavy load across the grass between the car and our tents.

Twenty minutes later, it was all in, with room for our tents, cases and sleeping bags. Ted noticed that our car was really low on the suspension, but it was fine. I agreed with him and said; "yes it is low, but not as low as it was when we came across on the ferry from Southampton the other day."

We walked across the grass weaving in and around the tents and vans. Brian said, "how about loading all the food too; we will leave early and stop for breakfast on the road. That way we can get out of Munich before the heavy morning traffic builds up with commuters."

That was what Ted and Jean were doing. They intended to leave at 5.30 Tony and I had no problem with that plan. We would have to be up at four-thirty to leave that early.

Brian said, "Alright, we'll plan on that, set your alarms so we can leave early and cover as much distance as as possible. Ted and Jean wanted us all of us to come for supper. They had a small oven on their camper, and she said she could cook a nice meal.

Brian asked me to go over to the car and get some vegetables, and two tins of soup. He also wanted me to bring over a can of potatoes if I found them. This would keep me busy for a while. I unpacked part of the trunk to pull out all of these items. I found everything and took it over.

As I gave them to her, I asked if I could help. She said, "No, thank you. I'm very happy to do this, I like making meals for people. I used to have to do this for my family and I loved it. It is a little difficult with this small kitchen in the van, but I'll manage. Supper should be ready at around seven-thirty."

Ted and Brian were content to play cards while Jean continued to get the supper ready. Tony and I decided to play a game of "Chess." We were unable to finish our game before dinner. We took our chairs and headed over to see what kind of glorious meal Jean had made. The table was set beautifully. There were place settings, napkins, and even wine glasses.

Ted was sitting at the head of the table and Brian right next to him; "You boys sit at either end of the table. This will be good for Jean; when she serves dinner as she will be near the stoves. We only have white wine, I hope that's alright with you boys?"

I said "No problem, I'm fine with that. What do you think, Tony?"

"It's fine with me, pour away." Ted said we should make a toast to Jean for cooking our fine supper. Jean stepped out with a large plastic bowl and said the salad was tossed with oil and vinegar, because that was all they had.

We said everything was wonderful. "Go ahead with the salad and I will join you shortly. I have to enter a few notes in my travel journal or I will forget some details."

The salad was amazing with Romaine Lettuce, tomatoes, onion, red peppers, grated cheese and mandarin segments. I've never had a salad anything like this before. It was very tasty. Jean joined us and asked who wanted dark meat, a leg, or a wing; as we were having roast chicken.

Tony asked for white meat; Ted and I wanted a leg.

Jean said that was perfect, as she liked wings. Remember we do not want to have food left over, so I do hope you all have a good appetite.

When Jean served us our meals, it was hard to believe what she had accomplished in such a confined space. There was chicken, potatoes, and peas with very nice gravy. We all enjoyed our meals and were talking about our plans for the next day. Ted and Jean wanted to leave at the same time as us, so hopefully we could all meet again.

In nearby Austria, they had seen a very nice campsite on the map. It was in the city of Vienna, where we were all heading. If we could all be ready to set out at the same time, we could stop for breakfast at the same place in the morning.

Tony and I insisted on taking everything over to the washroom and cleaning up for Jean. "Thank you, that's very nice, I will have coffee with a liqueur ready for you when you come back."

After completing the washing and drying, Tony asked me what Brian really liked about this couple, as it is clear he is a loner. "We are going to travel into Austria with them, but know for sure, they are not heading for Turkey or Singapore. I imagine this friendship will probably end in Austria and we will part ways."

When we returned to the van, Ted and Jean poured our coffee and placed a bottle of orange liqueur on the table saying. "This is what we use for sugar in our coffee." We did as she said and wow, it tasted really good. It was something new to me, but Tony had this before and he very enjoyed every sip of it.

Ted said, "Well folks, it is not late, but I think we should turn in, as we are setting out very early in the morning. You have tents, cases and bedding to pack into your car. We only have to retract the awning, put the table and chairs in our van and we are ready to go. We'll do this tonight, so it will be an easy start for us".

We thanked them for a great evening and a fantastic meal and headed for our tents. At this time of night, it was a very difficult path, even with a flashlight you had to be careful. Settling down for the night, l was wondering what it was going to be like packing and dismantling the tents, with flashlights to help us see.

I woke up to the sound of a car engine that seemed very close to my tent. I looked out and saw the camper van nearest to us was moving out. I could see directly across to Ted and Jean's; there was no sign of any lights over there yet. I saw by my watch, it was already 4.30 in the morning. I grabbed my flashlight, got dressed and ran to the washroom. When I came back I started packing. It did not take me very long. I started taking down the tent. Hopefully, Tony, Brian, Jean and Ted would be up soon.

Ted was now up; he drove his van to face us and turned on his head lights. Now it was easy for us to see what we doing. All we had to do was wake up Brian. Tony was coming out of his tent, so we should be all ready to leave soon. Brian's light was now on and we could see he was getting dressed. He took his time but we knew he'd be ready to go soon.

Tony went of to the washroom. When he returned, it did not take long for him to pack everything and put it in his backpack. Soon he was ready to get into the car. Brian came out holding his hands over his eyes and said. "What the hell is going on?"

Don't worry, Brian I said. "Ted has his van lights on us so we can see what we are doing. We are on schedule; it is four-thirty."

"Great thanks, Ted" he said, "Guys, give me a few minutes to wake and clean up, then I will join you at our car."

I asked Brian to take what he needed out of the tent and I would pack it all while he was gone. I knew he would be quite a while but I would easily have everything packed by the time he returned.

When Brian came out of the washroom, we had everything packed and in the car. Ted waited for him and then escorted him to our car. Ted had volunteered to lead us out of Munich, the Bavarian Forest and Germany. He was confident that if we followed him, this will be easy.

CHAPTER 16

Travelling out of the Bavarian capital at that early hour was great. We had avoided the rush hour so there was very little traffic. After driving for about 40 minutes, I saw the signs for the Autobahn. I was sure taking this fast motorway would have us in nearby Austria soon.

Ted didn't push his camper van too fast, as I had mentioned to him that our car is riding low. We needed to take care as we had a long way to go. After all we were going to Singapore and they were touring Europe. I wondered if Ted realized that we needed to stop soon for breakfast. We had to keep an eye out for a restaurant. I had to flash my headlights so he knew we wanted to stop.

Tony said we were very close the Autobahn from the position he had on the map. Then Ted signaled a left turn as we pulled into the parking lot. We landed at a small café that had just opened. It was now about six-thirty and we were hungry.

A very young German girl from behind the counter said in English, "Order at the counter, please".

I immediately went to the counter and asked how she knew we are English? She said "that was easy. Both the vehicles you came in have English or GB plates or stickers. Would you like tea or coffee?"

"I would like four coffees and one tea please."

"What do you want for breakfast?" "I would be happy with scrambled eggs and toast." Everyone liked that idea, so I ordered five orders scrambled eggs and toast.

The coffee was fresh and she poured four cups on the counter then she asked, "What type of tea would the gentleman like? We have good selection in a wooden box. Let me show him so he can choose."

I passed the big mahogany case to Brian and he picked Earl Grey. "Please take the one out you would like, I will bring a small pot and some hot water, sugar and milk for you."
    She told us there were no waiters and came from around the counter with the hot water. She dropped the tea bag in the small metal pot then poured the hot water to steep the tea.

Ted said, "It's not far now to the Autobahn, how far do you think it is to the Austrian border?"

"I'm not sure, but we will be sleeping in Austria tonight; how close to Vienna we get, depends on how well the traffic flows on the highway. Normally it is very good, but you never know what can happen on these high speed roads."

"I will try to stay at about 70 mph, if that is alright with Brian."

"Sure should be fine", he replies

The cafe had really old wooden panels from floor to ceiling with a blue chair rail. It had light brown painted walls with panels painted on to have them give the impression of raised panels. There were pictures in the panels of landscapes. The scenic pictures really added a distinctive character to such a small place.

There was now a constant stream of people who were just getting coffee coming in and out. They were all being handled in a very efficient manner. They must have been regulars as they all seemed to know the pretty young girl on a first name first name basis.

Our breakfasts were now ready and placed on the counter for us to collect. There was a good amount of scrambled eggs and large pieces of brown rye toast, with a few fried potatoes. Everyone agreed they were happy with their traditionally English breakfast.

The young girl came back and asked if everything was to our liking. We all nodded and said "very good."

Brian said, "Just give me the bill". "Ted argues "No, give the bill to me"

Tony looked at me and smiled. He knew he probably was going have a free breakfast, (he was supposed to be paying his way.) We wondered how much money Brian got from the banks in Munich. We knew he must have gone to a few every time he was alone. The fact that he was happy to impress everyone by paying for meals indicated that he surely had accumulated a large amount of

German marks. As per normal, his precious brown shoulder bag was with him hanging on his chair in his full view.

Ted asserted, "If you pay this, Brian, I will pay for lunch or supper if we don't have supper at a campsite." Brian agreed and settled the bill with cash," It had taken us about an hour to eat leisurely.

"To be fair", Tony says, "I will pay the tip for the young girl; she was very good to us." Brian handed Tony the bill and asked him to decide how much he wanted to tip for the great service.

We left the café at seven thirty and headed out onto the highway. Finally reaching the Autobahn about 15 minutes later, we noticed the highway was very busy, but the traffic was moving fast. It was peak hours for the commuters. We followed Ted at 80 mph which was okay, but not the speed I would have travelled at. The car seemed rock steady and we hoped she held up under this constant speed and heavy load.

The scenery was really alpine-like as we zigzagged through forests, over large viaducts and through the occasional tunnel. My worry was the muffler and the temperature of the engine. I kept a constant eye on the temperature gauges to ensure the engine didn't overheat. I was fairly sure that it would be alright in the early morning, with the cool temperatures.

Brian was happy, since at this rate, we would be at the border before midday. Tony was following our route well and said, "By my calculations we should be at the border around lunchtime. This was allowing for an average speed of 60 mph."

This was easily achievable, even taking into consideration our slow start from the café to the highway. Tony seemed excellent at assessing time and distance as long as there were no unexpected circumstances.

We travelled very well for over three hours; then we had to slow down to 40 mph as the traffic became very heavy and slow. We came to a complete stop. We weren't far from the border and there was nothing we could do, as there were no alternative exits. Tony said, "There aren't many small roads off this highway. How would we advise Ted that we are going to make a detour?" The traffic started to pick up speed again and Tony declares, "Our estimated time to reach the border is now about 1:30 pm."

Brian states, "That's 30 minutes from now, is that at 70 mph?"

Tony replies, "Yes, that's what I calculated"

We reached the border right on the time, as Tony had predicted, but there is a huge line up. That meant we would be here for a while. Jean got out of her vehicle and walked over to us saying, "The officials are looking for something as there are police all over the place."

Brian immediately asked "do you have any idea what they are looking for?"

Jean replied, "I'm not really sure, when I get closer I will let you know."

Brian seemed nervous and got out of our car to see what was happening. He walked towards the front of the long line of cars. It was not like him to leave his shoulder bag on the seat in the car with us and walk away. Tony said that he had to be concerned to walk towards the border.

Alan, "I will let you know when Brian starts walking back." There were probably 30 cars in front of us when he was halfway down the line. Jean was now out of their car and quickly on her way to catch up with him. When she did catch up, they stopped to discuss what they could see. Many people were walking down the road and some were coming back to their cars.

Tony commands "Alan, open the bag and have a look to see what is in his shoulder bag." I could see them walking towards the border." I opened the bag and found many envelopes of cash. There were English pounds, German marks and French francs. I tell Tony that our earlier reasoning was right. There was an enormous amount of money. I zipped up the bag and put it back quickly before Brian could catch us.

Brian was probably nervous about this money. If customs searches the car and finds all that money, they will be curious as to why he is carrying so much cash in several currencies. It would be very interesting to see how he explains the amount, as at some borders you are limited on the amount of currency you can bring into a country.

Tony remarks that there seemed to be a lot of action down there and everyone was running back. Then we heard shots fired. Brian was returning and did not run, but was walking much quicker than I have ever seen him move. Jean was keeping up with him. She went back into the van.

Brian gets into our car a little out of breath, and seems somewhat relieved at what he had seen. I ask him what had happened. "We heard the shots."

"The police were opening all the trunks of the cars", when a man jumped out of a van and made a run for it. They shouted at him to stop, but he kept running. I guess they shot him. Then the police officers told us all to return back to our cars. We will be getting across the border very soon. They would get everyone through quickly now to speed traffic."

He was right, soon we were moving and in a very short time, customs was asking us for our passports and where we were heading. I said Singapore. He just looked at our passports, smiled and handed them back, "Good luck."

Ted was ahead and stopped on the side of the road to wait for us. Soon we were back on the road, but now we were only travelling at 70 mph, as the speed limits in Austria were limited, unlike the Autobahn which had no speed limit.

Tony said, "Do we have any plans for a stop as I would like to have a drink and use a toilet?"

Brian answered, "Hang on, because Jean and Ted mentioned paying for our lunch, and that should be soon. Now that we have crossed the border, our first main goal for the day is achieved and we can eat."

We saw a sign for a service station about ten kilometres or eight miles ahead. That was about 5 minutes from where we were. Ted must have seen the road sign, because as we passed by, he put on his right indicator. There was no sign of him slowing down, but I would assume from this, that we were still stopping. We should fill up with petrol as we were getting low on fuel. Just as I thought, he was indicating his turn, so we must have been very close to the service centre. Pulling up and parking right outside of the service station entrance, we noticed that there were very few people. We used the facilities,

We then all walked back and found the fast food service section. Ted suggested he buy a large pizza and some soft drinks. We agreed. He returned with the biggest pizza I have ever seen, saying, "This is a party veggie pizza".

As he was not sure about what everyone wanted, he decided on the veggie. He also had paper plates, napkins and a cold can of cola for each of us.

Brian commented "That veggie pizza was a great idea".

Brian now suggested that we get going because we have to fuel up and get to Vienna before dark. As we looked at the fuel pump reading, Ted commented, "Wow. Brian your "American monster" sure does soak up the gas;" Yes, it does because of the weight we are carrying. When we travel over 60 mph, it is well beyond its economical speed and just guzzles up fuel."

CHAPTER 17

When we got back on the road, the car started to bump around, and I had a suspicion we were going to have a suspension problem by the time we got to the Austrian capital of Wien or Vienna. Brian noticed that we were wandering a bit every time we changed lanes and wanted to know why. The car's handling was not good. I told him that it was hard to keep going in a straight line which meant one side could be weak, or maybe a spring was broken. We would soon need more repairs to our Ford.

Brian was not happy, and his patience was running short with the car, and now I wondered how far this car would take us. Brian, being very upset, said he was going to contact the man, who was supposed to be a reliable friend when he got back to England, and he was going to give him a piece of his mind. Then he would contact everyone he knew to let them know how untrustworthy this guy was.

These were going to be our last few nights with Ted and Jean, because they were not intending to go on into Yugoslavia. We might go through Hungary, but if so, we will needed transit visas. Perhaps we could get them while in the capital.

As we drove into Vienna, we felt every bump on the road. Brian said, "I hope we can make it to a campsite, I would like to take everything out of the car and check out what's happening, Alan."

We pulled into a very modern campsite behind Ted. It had a two storey brick building in the middle of the site, by a river. The roads all around the campsite were paved; and sections were marked off with posts for each car or camper. It did not seem busy and the washroom facilities were right near the office in the middle of the treed field.

Brian got out and entered with Ted, Tony followed them, while Jean exited the van and came over to my side of the car.

"What do you think of this site, Alan?"

"Well Jean I think its great, but judging by how new the building and facilities are, it's probably expensive. The grounds are somewhat empty, so we may able to make a cash deal."

A short time later, the two men came out smiling, with keys for the facilities and permits for spaces next to each other right by the Danube River. Brian got in the car and said to me, "Follow behind Ted."

I hoped that the suspension took a longer time to repair, that may be unfair but that would give us more time here in this beautiful position by the river. Tired from driving, we could enjoy the city. As we set up the tents in our camping space, the sun was shining; making it just perfect for us.

It would be very nice to spend more than a few days at this campsite, as it was the best place we had seen yet. Brian was helpful and seemed keen to clear the car. Taking everything out, we looked to see if the car came up as the weight came off.

As soon as we were all set up, Brian asked me to jack the car up and take a look at the suspension. I had to remove the spare wheel to get the jack out. The car was so low that it wasn't easy to get the jack under any part of the back end. Tony went to find a piece of wood or something flat, maybe a piece concrete or a plank he could use as a lever. He returned with piece of plywood, very rough and about half an inch thick.

The jack just fit under the car on the plywood. I started to jack up the car slowly, and hoped the plywood held. I had to lift it up to the maximum and hoped it would give me enough space to see underneath.

Ted came over and asked, "Did you manage to see what the problem was yet".

"Well I have just jacked it as high as it will go, but it's only just lifted the wheels off the ground. It is not enough to see what is wrong."

Ted suggested putting something under the car to support it. He did not trust the jack to hold up safely. I told him I would use a mirror and a flashlight to see what I could. After getting it high enough, it was easy to see that the leaf springs were finished and needed replacing. They were still straight but should have an arch in them, even under this heavy load. It is not a hard job, but we would need to put the car on a hoist in a garage to replace them.

Brian unhappily asked what this would cost. I told him that I had no idea, but it was not a long job. We just had to find a garage that could get the springs to fit them. Ted mentioned that he saw some nearby.

Jean came over and asked Brian to supper. Brian told me I should get something to eat in town, because he was sure I would like to explore the town with Tony. Brian gave me some money and mentioned that it would be a good idea to find out where the Hungarian Embassy or Consulate for England was, because if we decided to go that way we would need transit visas for passage through the country.

CHAPTER 18

Considering that it was not late, Tony and I decided to walk down the street in the direction we came to see what we could find. Ted suggested he drive us in his van, but Tony and I wanted to walk, so we set off for the main street to explore, eat, and have a beer.

When we reached the street, we saw that the shops were open, and traffic was heavy at the end of a working day. We walked for about 10 minutes and saw the first garage; it was only a filling station. We decided to try our luck and see if anyone spoke English or could direct us to a repair garage.

The young man running the next station did not speak English, I drew a picture of a car, and even though it wasn't very good, he smiled and said, "I cannot fix car." He walked us out to the street and pointed down the road saying, walking would get us to a garage in five minutes. We thanked him and set off again. We soon saw one, it was an Audi garage.

"Alan, you know Audi is part of Volkswagen, it's going to be very expensive just like the one in Munich"

"You're right Tony, let's go farther up the street, we may find a smaller or a less expensive garage."

We walked down the first street. It was not looking good so we headed back to the main road to see what the next street had. On the main road, we came to a tavern and decided to try our luck in there, have a beer, something to eat; then find a garage. This tavern was more like a restaurant with many tables and waitress service. At the entrance there was a hostess and we had to wait to be shown to a table. I noticed that there were a lot of very nice looking waitresses, and I had a few smiles from them, so I winked and got some nicer smiles in return.

The place with its nice tablecloths and fancy lighting looked expensive. We are hungry and thirsty; we just hoped English was spoken here. A beautiful blond approached us and asked in an accent if we would like a table. She was a young Swedish girl who spoke English; I asked how good her English was, since we had no knowledge of her native language. She said it was not a problem for her, since she could speak English, French and German.

"What can I help you with? She asked.

"We need a good garage that's not too expensive, to repair our car."

"That would have to be on the other side of town", she said. There was a young man formerly with a big garage who has now started his own business. It's a long way from here, approximately ten miles."

"Very good but we cannot drive that far as our car does not really have any suspension."

She told us where the garage was, and that the guy would come and get it since he had a tow truck. He tows breakdowns in all the time, and fixes them. He is a very good mechanic and not expensive like the dealership garages nearby.

"Okay, perhaps he can help us. We have a big two-tone American Ford car, with a white top and red bottom, parked in the campsite by the river."

She replied, "No problem. I know where that is; I will call him and send him over to tow your car tonight"

We followed her to a table, where she left us with menus and told us the waitress would be right with us. We looked at the menu and found that it was too expensive for our budget. Our joint agreement was to have a beer and leave, and have a look for somewhere else to eat.

The waitress came and in a very clear English accent asked what we would like, and we answered only two beers please. We would prefer Stella's if you have them."

"No problem" she then leaned down close and said quietly, "Since you have realized the food here is expensive, just go out to the street, turn right and go down the next road. To your right, you will get the best burgers in town for a reasonable price."

I commented, "You're an absolute doll, where are you from?"

"I'm from Wolverhampton, England and my father works here."

"I'm Alan and from Southampton, and we're travelling to Singapore by car." Tony is from Totton.

"Wow that is one big journey, I will fetch your beers; you must be thirsty." She smiles at me and leaves.

"This girl has really taken an instant liking to you, Alan," Tony noticed.

"I never really paid that much attention, but she seems keen to talk to us. I thought she was just being nice, and a friendly waitress. Well I will play along and we will see what happens when she returns."

She was short with long dark hair in a ponytail and a very pretty round face, beautiful completion with hazel eyes and a smile that would light up a room. She was my type of girl for sure. All the restaurant's waitresses were dressed in black slacks and white blouses, many of them smiling were at me.

Tony comments, "The food is expensive but there are lots of nice waitresses."

As soon she arrived with the beers, I asked her name. Her answer was, "My name is Lisa, I will be your waitress," Then she asked where we were staying.

"We are at a campsite by the Isar River, overlooking the Alps," I replied.

"That's great, I love camping and that has to be the best camp site in town, I know it well."

I replied, "I have no objection if you want to come and visit us I'm sure you finish late, so you will not be over tonight."

A few minutes later, Lisa came back smiling and said "I will finish my shift at 9.00. Can I drop by tonight and see you later when I finish."

"Sure you can, it is a good walk from here."

"I have a car, so there is no problem getting up to that camp site"

"Good, we will tell Brian we have a visitor tonight. He will not mind as he usually plays cards with some friends he met in Munich".

"To find us look for 3 tents right by the river. All the tents entrances face each other. We are right next to a camper van; that's Brian's friend's van. It has a big two coloured awning."

"A fellow from a car garage is going to pick up our tonight.

The hostess gave us the name of the young car repair guy, we knew that Brian would be happy if he could get it repaired for a good price, and he could it get back to us in a day or two. He is unhappy about delays and repairs."

"Great, we will talk more tonight; I must get back to work." She smiles at me again, winks, touches my shoulder and hurries off.

Tony said, "If she comes over tonight you're probably going to get lucky from the way she was behaving with you. Brian has done you a big favour giving you your own tent."

"I hope we have some luck with the burgers. I am very hungry."

We enjoyed our drinks and paid Lisa; then we left to look for the burger place she had told us about. When we left, Lisa smiled at me again saying "see you later."

Outside the bar, heading for the burger shop, Tony said, "wow, she really has a crush on you Alan. I suggest that you just play it cool."

"Sure but I will not expect too much, we have just met and we will have to spend some time getting to know each other."

"You are forgetting that she knows we are travelling and we may not be here very long. I know she has her eyes on you."

It seemed a lot of people in the lineup understood English and some of the girls were looking and giggling.

Tony smiled back at them and asked what they were doing later. They answered "why, are you lonely tonight. Your friend seems to be set up. We would love to come and see you, where are you staying?"

"I'm leaving for Singapore tomorrow", so I have to say no thanks girls."

They continued and asked, "Where are you flying from?"

"I am leaving early by car," No more was said and we went to the burger bar to order our cheese burgers and leave.

When we walked back, eating our burgers and drinking a coke, I ask why he put the girls off with that story about leaving early for Singapore.

"I know you may probably have a chance with Lisa and they could have messed up the evening for you. The girls are way too young to be sensible and discreet. I hope you would do the same for me if a similar situation arose."

"I sure would, you're a real friend, and I owe you one."

"I would like to go out for a drink with her if she is willing. I will see how things go from there. You never know, she may just want to see our campsite."

"It will still be light when you leave, so your plans could work, because by the time you return it will be dark and you can discreetly do what ever you both want."

"I will shower, shave and dress in my best gear. That should impress her, after meeting me today in just t-shirt and shorts."

"She should really respect that kind of effort, knowing that when camping you don't carry much in the way of smart clothing. We are always in shorts and t-shirts and some times only swimming trunks".

Upon our arrival at the camp site, it was immediately noticeable, that there were a lot more campers now. Brian was with Ted and Jean, they were chatting and he looks quite content. Perhaps he was winning at cards. I immediately told everyone that I had a date coming over tonight.

Brian quickly asked, "Does she know where we are going and that you will not be here for long?"

"I will tell her tonight. I have also arranged for a young mechanic to come over tonight to take the car. He has a tow truck and will take the car, fix it for a reasonable price and bring it back. We will make a deal with him and I was told he would be fair. If you pay cash, you can be sure of a quick efficient job just as Herman did for us in Munich.

"What do you think Brian?" "Everyone you have dealt with so far has been fair. You can sort it out with him and strike a good deal before you set off on a date with your new acquaintance."

"It should be alright as Lisa does not finish work until 9.00.

Soon, the guy with the truck pulls in and drives right over to us. It is not hard to find a red and white American coupe. The fellow stops, gets out of his tow truck and in an accent states his English is not good. He points to the car and gestures about lifting it up to look under the back end. He wants to take a closer look at the suspension problem. Very quickly, he jacked up the car with a small trolley jack and was under it with a flash light. He came out from under the car and stated he could fix it and would bring it back tomorrow night. He would charge about 100 marks.

I said that sounded fine but how much for cash, no bill? He answered ninety marks. Brian heard this and said that was fine. He can take it; I will pay half now and the rest when he returns with the repaired car. Brian took out the cash paid him the deposit. The young man hitched up our car and left.

I would assume that Brian must now have quite a bit of cash, as he had been taking it daily from the local banks, He seemed to be freely giving it out, especially paying direct cash for the car.

It is getting late, so I took a shower and got ready, then waited for Lisa.

Ted and Jean were interested in my date. "How did you meet her? And where is she from?" "She is from Wolverhampton and a waitress in a bar we were in today", I answered.

"I will know more about her tonight after we go on our date. I really do hope she shows up" I said.

Tony said "Alan is being very apprehensive about the entire situation, but from where I was sitting, watching her reactions, she will be here."

To Tony's surprise, Brian pulled out a mark, and bet that she comes and would be here before nine-twenty. Ted bet a mark she would be here by 9.15. Tony exclaimed, I was only joking, but will take the money and bet a mark on a nine-ten arrival. Jean says she will be the banker, and suggests Alan should take all the money if they are all wrong. Everyone agreed that this was fair.

When I returned from the shower, they were all playing cards, and there was change on the table. I now know why Brian likes Ted and Jean; they enjoy playing poker for small change. As I passed by, Jean looked up and smiled saying "you look very presentable;' I do hope she respects the effort." The men agreed and wished me the "best of luck".

I went over to my tent to complete my journal for the day leaving space for the night ahead, and hoping it was going to be interesting. Tony came over and asked me to join him for a drink, as it was almost 9.00 pm. He was looking towards the entrance for Lisa to enter the campsite at 9.10, so he could collect all the money.

I told him that if she comes right from work at nine and jumps in her car, she can be here before 9.10. It's only a three minute car ride from there and I assume that she will finish early and change at work, so she may leave on time. We were all sitting around the table. As I watched them play poker I noticed Tony had a good hand.

We heard a car horn and saw Lisa in a very nice Volkswagen Golf stop right by us and its 9.10 pm. Tony jumped up, exclaiming, "I win the bet"!!!!!

"Ok said Brian, put your cards on the table, let us meet Lisa, then we can continue our game." Brian told Jean to give the money in the "pot" to Tony as Lisa arrived right on 9.10, just as he predicted.

Lisa got out of her car and looked stunning with her short skirt, tank top, hair down and no makeup. She came straight over to me and remarked that I look great and suggested I give her a kiss on the cheek and then introduce her to "the gang." before we head out.

"Alan, I have taken the liberty of arranging something, I hope you don't mind."

"That's great." I did quick introductions. "There is Brian, who I am driving for, and Tony, our passenger. This is Ted and his wife Jean; we met them on route.

There were smiles of approval. Lisa then commented to me that she had arranged a great place to take me for a meal.

My heart was beating like a drum, and I couldn't wait to get started. We got into the car and left. I felt apprehensive but at the same time extremely excited. I waved good bye and jumped into Lisa's Volkswagen. As soon as we reached the entrance, I asked her to stop for a moment.

"Lisa I have to tell you that I'm nervous, as this is a new experience for me. We have only known each other for a very short time and we are heading out on a dinner date."

She replied, "This is not a usual situation for me, and I have never done anything like this before. I have to tell you. I found you very attractive and charming the second I met you. You are such a good looking man with a kind nature, relaxed attitude and I just decided this was a very respectable man that has not tried to manhandle me or ask for a date, like all the young men usually do. At the bar you were noticed by almost all of the waitresses, and they were curious to know more about this handsome young man. I was the lucky one to serve you."

I felt much better; I leaned over and kissed her on the cheek. She immediately put her arm around my neck and kissed me on the lips. "How far is this place we are going to?"

"The traffic is not heavy, so we should be there in around 20 minutes. We do not want to eat too late. This place is open late so we have plenty of time."

With the mischievous look on her face, it was obvious she was up to something, but what; she is a lovely girl and extremely pleasant and desirable to me.

On the highway, traffic was moving very fast for about ten minutes; we pulled off and turned onto a road going down by a lake. There was no sign of a bar or restaurant, but I see a very big house with a triple garage. The lake was only a short walk away. We stopped on the drive and she looked at me, smiled and puts her arms around my neck and kissed me again. She then confessed that this is where she lives with her parents, and they are away at the present time. "My father is the ambassador at the UK embassy in Vienna. The housekeeper has made dinner for us."

"What do you think of me now?"

"I am pleasantly surprised, and you are so nice; I wish I was staying in Austria a lot longer. I must leave Austria and head for Yugoslavia in a day or two. Let us go and enjoy dinner.'

Lisa explained that the house keeper only spoke a small amount of English. On entering the house, I figured her parents were very wealthy. (Later I learned the house belonged to Great Britain,) I took off my shoes and she said, "No need really, Alan. All the floors are hardwood and unless it's winter or wet we do not bother."

The house keeper smiled, and led us into the dinning room. A beautiful table was set with place settings for two. The house was old with wood panelling on the walls, and beautiful art work. There was a huge brass chandelier over the dining room table. We sat facing each other, and Lisa just beamed, non-stop. The housekeeper spoke briefly to Lisa and then headed for the kitchen. We started with the salad on the table. Lisa then said. "We are going to have Sheppard's pie; I hope that's alright with you."

"That will be a treat, but doing anything with you would be nice. This is a real pleasure for me since I have been living in a tent for a week. I gambled and started to play footsies with her. She grinned and looked at me in such away that I knew it was going to be an interesting evening. We enjoyed the salad; then the house keeper served the Sheppard's pie.

"The house keeper has to go soon, as her son is picking her up. She stayed late as a personal favour to get our meal ready." Lisa continued, "I called her from work today. After I spoke with you, I just decided you were the gentleman for me."

The Sheppard's pie was excellent and when we finished, Lisa asked, if I would like to take a stroll down to the lake.

"That would be great. It was a lovely location and a beautiful warm evening. "I would love to see the lake."

As we walked down to the lake she said, "I cannot believe how nice you are; how long do you think this journey will take?"

"Originally the plan was six to eight weeks, but we have had a few problems and have been held up, so we are not sure now"

On the small boat dock, with our arms wrapped around each other, she said with a big smile, "I do not want to lose touch with you and would like very much if you would stay for breakfast."

"That's not a problem, what time do you have to be at work tomorrow?" I asked.

"I start at noon, so we do not have to get up early in the morning."

"Lisa I will send you post cards and you can track my journey across Europe and into the Middle East."

We now kiss very passionately, and slowly walk back to the house. "Lisa you are a charming girl, but I have to tell you I was not really expecting to stay overnight. I would have brought my washroom bag, had I known that I might be staying over night."

"That will not be problem; we can most certainly drive back to your campsite to get what you need. I hope you will get more than your toothbrush as you will love the house and may like to stay a little longer. Having met you I have already been thinking about moving back to England, where I have an aunt who I have lived with before, when I was in university. Tell me about your education and background.

"In 1967, I completed a boatbuilding apprenticeship. For over five years, I have worked for myself doing many things, selling life insurance, doing furniture restoration, installing suspended ceilings for a year, been an exhibition installer and now I am driving Mr. Turner to Singapore."

"My father will would like to meet you as he has always talked about getting a boat for the lake."

"Lisa, I will be heading home soon after the journey is completed, and will give you my address in England." The drive back was very quick. She knew where she was going. It was about 11.30 pm when we arrived at the campsite to pick up my things.

I scribbled a note reading. 'Will be back some time in the morning, Alan' and put it under the wiper blade on Ted's van. This was the best place for it. It was very visible and would be found for sure. I was positive that they would all be talking about us at breakfast. Lisa was outside the car and watching me place the note.

She walked up to me and said. "We should go now, or I will want to get into your tent with you." I told her to drive steady and not to be in so much of a hurry, as we will have all night to relax and enjoy each other. She smiled and said "Ok you can drive if you would like to, I'm sure you drive stick, right?"

"Sure do. When do your parents return home?"

"I better drive, but I will drive slower. My parents are away for another couple of days, so you can stay with me as long as you like. They are liberally minded, and I know they would love to meet you."

When we arrived back at the house, it was extremely dark and there were no lights anywhere. She opened the garage door from a key pad by the front gate. Once the door closed, she put her arms around my neck and kissed me saying, "I've waited long enough." We kissed passionately again, before she led me into the house and straight upstairs to her bedroom. She had an on-suite bathroom and told me to make myself comfortable, and with a really sexy smile, said "I will return shortly."

I brushed my teeth , undressed and laid on her bed, and when she came back, she walked in with a lovely negligee, so thin, she might as well been naked. "Wow, you sure know how to please a man. You look absolutely fabulous," I said.

She replied. "You are as I imagined you would be naked. You must workout a lot as you are in good shape."

It was to be a fabulous night for both of us. We made love all night long. I did not wake up until eight, which was very unusual for me. Lisa was not next to me when I awoke.

I called out her name and she walked in, beaming and wearing a beautiful negligee style house coat. She said, "You are the best thing that has ever happened to me, I love you." This was a shock, as I was nervous of the whole situation. I had not met her parents, but stayed with their daughter overnight.

I whispered, loud enough for her to hear. "Get that beautiful negligee off now." She did in a flash, and of course she was nude. Quickly she gets back into bed with me and I mentioned. "We can have breakfast much later." We had breakfast at 10.00. She said, "We must leave at eleven, so I can get you back to your friends. I have to get to work early so I will have to change at work."

Lisa, you would look terrific in anything. I love long hair and a girl that can pull her hair back and still look good." She kissed me and said, "You better stop those comments or I will be very late for work".

CHAPTER 19

As we drove back into Vienna, we passed the Imperial Palace, the Hofburg complex and Freud Museum. The traffic got much heavier, so it was not such a quick trip. "When will I see you again?" Lisa asked.

"I will be over for a drink in the afternoon. Do you have a break during your shift? We can meet then.

"Yes I will be off at 3.30 for an hour."

"Great, can we go for a walk somewhere and have a drink?" I asked.

"We can go to a very nice place by the river. It will be busy, but that's normal for this time of year in all the scenic places."

Arriving at the campsite at eleven-thirty, we found, Brian, Ted and Jean sitting at the table under the camper awning having coffee. Tony was not there and I could see the tents were closed.

Lisa got out of the car then came around and and kissed me, saying, "Bye everyone, and see you later darling" They all saw and heard this. She waved goodbye and, she drove away

"Where is Tony?" I asked" and Brian told me had gone to find the British Embassy. He needed to renew his passport and hopefully find the Hungarian one. Embassies are usually close to each other in most cities. He left at eight, so he should be back soon. I am sure he will be interested to know if your girlfriend's father knows anyone who can help him with his passport"

"I will ask her this afternoon when I meet at her break time". Brian commented, "You have another date, already?" I replied, "Yes, We arranged to meet during her lunch break at 3.30 for an hour".

I got into my tent and entered my last few adventures into my journal, as I had many interesting events to record. This took a few hours.

When Tony returned, he came over to my tent and said. "I was correct, from the time I saw the expression on her face in the bar."

"Did you have any luck with your passport? Her father works at the British Embassy, and he may know someone who can help speed up your passport application."

Brain was listening, and immediately said "Yes and we need the car repair sped up to, I hope we can leave tomorrow." This was the disadvantage of being too close, as someone could hear all your conversations.

"Alan, ask Lisa if she is sure she help us with the paperwork."

"Don't worry I am sure Lisa will be able to contact someone. Her father must be well connected in the Embassy. "Great, do you think we can go for a drink, and you can ask her before she breaks for lunch? I am sure she would be delighted to see you earlier. The drink will be on me. It will be worth it to get my passport and continue with you and Brian."

Tony and I headed for the bar at 12.30 and hoped she was not too shocked to see me again, especially since I wanted a favour. As we walked to the bar, Tony wanted to know more details of our date.

"We slept together, as you assumed all along. She has been alone for two years. I came along, and now I want to stay in touch with her. She wants to go back to England when we leave, so we can connect up again," I said. "Wow, you found a steady girlfriend in Austria. You must have really impressed her last night, for her to want to continue a long distance relationship."

I explained that the main thing was that I promised to drive Brian to Singapore, and at the moment that is my commitment. She understands this, but said I can stay with her as long as I want. Lets hope the car is delayed at least another day, and we can have another night together."

When we arrived at the bar entrance, the hostess instantly recognized me and said, "Wait, I will put you at one of Lisa's tables. She has some great news for you." Now I'm very curious. Tony says. "Well this is great I will get the news first hand". When we sat at the table, I couldn't see her, so we waited. Tony was amused; two seconds later, Lisa arrived and said, "Hi darling. You are early, shall I ask for the rest of the day off?"

"No Lisa, just give us the good news and bring us two Stellas please".

"Well, love of my life, the news is, the hostess knows about us and has arranged for your car to be delayed, so I can pick you up right from work tonight. You will be staying another day." She came close to me and whispered in my ear, "straight from here tonight to my bedroom."

"That is terrific news for me. Brian isn't going to be very happy staying longer in Vienna. Lisa, can I ask you a favour? "Do you know anyone at the embassy who can get Tony's passport sorted a little faster, and do you know where the Hungarian Embassy is located?"

"Sure, but we will have to go at three-thirty in the afternoon on my break, so we can sort it out. Let me get those beers". Tony was glad because he wanted to continue with me to Singapore". If his passport was not ready Brian would not want to stay any longer than necessary. Lisa returned with the beers and asked, "Can you stay till 3.30 or will you come back later?"

"We will come back later, as the food here is too expensive; we will walk to the burger place for something to eat." Tony asked, "Would you like another beer?" as he was paying. The thought of getting his passport quicker was worth treating me to another beer. Our being here would surely bring another smile to Lisa's face. Tony asked "Will I be invited to the wedding" "What wedding, I asked sarcastically, knowing he was joking. "The thought had been on my mind, as Lisa seemed to be everything I ever wanted. I couldn't tell her that yet, as we had only known each other for twenty-four hours. I had visions of her following us into Yugoslavia."

"Great, another beer would be good; you know I will never refuse a cold beer on a hot summer day, especially knowing that I do not have to drive for awhile. What could be better?" Tony saw

Lisa and held his glass up; she came right over and he ordered two more beers.

She smiled again and said "Great, are you staying to wait for me?"

"Sorry no. Just one more beer, then we will go for a burger." We decided not to say anything to Brian about the car as he would be suspicious as to how we knew of the delay. We will let him worry a little more. He won't be happy when the car is not back tonight as we promised.

All the waitresses went by one at a time, and grinned at me, and I had to wonder how much Lisa has told them about us. As if Tony read my thoughts, he said, "you know girls talk a lot to each other about their love lives, it's just a normal thing with them."

When we got to the burger shop, it was not too busy. We sat on the bar stools to eat our burgers. Tony commented "Alan you are very lucky everything is going so well for you, and there need to worry about anything. Brian is not going anywhere without you. He will not find anyone with your skills and knowledge of cars. My good fortune is to have met a great travel buddy like you."

"Thanks Tony I feel the same way as you, and we really have the situation under control with Brian. My thoughts are very simple, if I decide to go on alone for any reason, I will travel back home with you."

"Alan, I have my concerns about you and Lisa. Will she understand when the time comes for you to leave; this girl is so smitten with you. I have never seen a girl become so attached to anyone in such a short time."

"Well, she knows that the delay on the car is only a bonus, and we will be gone in a day or two," I said." What did she whisper in your ear at the bar? I saw a smirk on your face that you could not hide?" "Very simple, Tony, there will be no supper before bed tonight." Seeing his puzzlement, I continued, "In simple terms, we will go straight to her bedroom from work. I do hope the housekeeper isn't there."

"Don't give me any more intimate details, you lucky devil."

"Now you know why I said that we will have supper at the camp site tonight." Behind the counter, we saw a nice coffee maker, so we decided to have a cappuccino each to wash down the rest of our burgers.

CHAPTER 20

Our coffees were great; Tony smiled and pointed to the door as two beautiful blondes walked into the burger place. I told him that they looked Scandinavian, as they had lovely natural blond hair. We would not have had a chance with them, even if they spoke English. They looked completely out of our league.

Tony turned and looked at them with a big smile, and they smiled back in return. He turned back to me and said. "They have just made my day smiling at me like that. Before he had a chance to say any more, one of them came over to him and said. "So what part of England are you from?"

Tony was in shock and stutters. "S-Southampton."

"OK but where is that in England? "They asked.

"It's southeast of London on the coast, right opposite France, and across the Channel from Le Harve. It is the home of the Titanic, Queen Mary

The Pilgrim's Mayflower, plus the British Spitfire and Tiger Moth".

"We are from Stockholm and are studying here for the summer. You both look like you are on holiday."

"We are on a journey which will end in Singapore"

"So are you flying out soon," they queried.

"No we are driving all the way."

"Wow, are you serious? Do you know how far that is and how dangerous a journey like that would be?"

I replied, "Yes, I am being paid to drive an artist there. My name is Alan and my companion is Tony."

"It's very nice to meet you. I am Sasha, this Angelica. (Sasha looked to be the eldest.)

"We are camped by the river and are heading to Yugoslavia tomorrow."

"We know where that is, we may drop in tonight, would that be alright?" Tony answered, "Fine, but Alan has an important rendezvous arranged and will leave at nine-fifteen.

Making our way back to the bar to meet Lisa, Tony said, "Wow that was nice, I wonder if they will come tonight. It's a shame you have a date with Lisa. I think we might have a chance with these two girls tonight, but I'll see what I can do, if they turn up."

The time was 3.15; Lisa should be ready. We were only a few metres away from the bar when we heard a car horn. It was Lisa; she pulled up right by us. When we got into the car, she told us that she had spoken to her boss and told him that she had to do some important work at the embassy for her father, so he let her go a few minutes early. It's not very far, and I have a pass to get in and park on the grounds for free."

"After what you told me at the bar, I think I will have my supper at the camp site tonight. Lisa said, grinning, "I know what you mean. I am looking forward to it."

We approached two big white wrought iron gates surrounding the embassy. A security guard came to the car asking, "Who do you have with you today, madam?"

"They are English. Alan, my boyfriend and Tony, his friend who wants to get his passport replaced. Is Jim in his office? I need his help"

"Wait here I will call him for you".

He returned and told her. "Park in your father's spot, Jim will come down to meet you. Have a nice day."

Jim Craddock came down to meet us. This nicely dressed English gentleman said. "Let me take you right to the office where we can get Tony's new passport." Tony was thrilled; "this is terrific I never would have imagined such good service."

Lisa was quick to say. "You can thank Alan for your good fortune." She turned, and gave me a kiss when Jim had his back to us. He led us into the building.

It was a wonderful old building. It has very high ceilings with huge cornices and very high baseboards. The floor was highly polished hardwood. The corridor has many doors with names of people written on them in nice wooden frames. Jim opened a door ahead of us saying, "This is Mrs. Andrews, our office manager." Lisa turned to Tony saying, "You go in; I want to show Alan my father's office."

Jim said to us, "I hope your journey goes well and you enjoy your stay in Austria." Tony goes in the office, and Lisa takes my hand saying, "Alan, come this way, Tony will be a while."

Down the corridor in the direction we came, past the entrance we turned into a small area with a staircase. We went up to another short corridor and she quickly pulled me into the first door; so speedily, that I never saw the name. She closed the door and started kissing me. Responding to her was easy, I grabbed her bottom with both hands, between the passionate kissing, saying "Darling, this is not the place to do this, let us wait till tonight"

Alan you are a real gentleman, and I can't help but think how lucky I am to know you. I have to ask you, would you consider ending your journey now, and maybe Tony can take over for you."

"I'm sorry Lisa but I want to complete this journey because to me it's going to be a great personal achievement. I have a journal and on completing this adventure, I will one day write a book. The story would be great to tell our children, do you not agree?"

"What a statement Alan. I am crazy about you but I am not even thinking of a commitment at this level. Even though at 27 years old, I should be thinking like that. My parents would love to meet you. I will be in England waiting for you when you return, that is my commitment."

"What about your plans to work here in a bank, it seemed very important to you to get out of the bar and start a nice regular job."

"That's before I met you; now my life goals have changed."

"I will be on the road to Singapore for another six weeks or more."

"Alan even another 6 weeks is nothing, when you consider I have been on my own for two years, getting over a break up, and looking for a young man just like you. Let's go back down and see if Tony has achieved what he wanted." We met Tony downstairs. He was very happy with his new passport. Now he could legally continue travelling with us.

"Rush hour" traffic in Vienna was very heavy; however Lisa made it back to work on time, even after dropping us off.

CHAPTER 21

When we got back to the campsite, Tony asked, "What happened in Lisa's dad's office? "Nothing too much, she was really affectionate.

"Alan you really are getting serious with this girl, are you sure you do not want to stay here with her, I can continue with Brian if you stay"

"Strange you should say that. That was what Lisa wanted me to do. But my mind is set on completing this journey. It is a challenge and I would like to complete this project on which I made a commitment."

"Great I wouldn't really want to go on without you, as I do not think I could handle Brian like you. As for fixing the car on the road, I know nothing about these things. It would be foolish for me to continue on with him."

"We have to consider that Brian is still pulling money from a number of bank accounts that he has. I would be suspicious of that; you must understand that once in Turkey and heading into the Middle East, his access to be banks will be limited. I am sure he is building up his funds for that part of the journey."

"Your biggest problem is making sure he secures that money, and he does not display to anyone that he is carrying a huge amount of cash. Just enjoy your romance with Lisa. Whatever happens with Brian, we will decide what we have to do between us."

This statement from Tony made me feel very confident. It showed that we were going to stick together no matter what happens on route.

Soon we reached the little side street that passes right by our burger spot. There were all kinds of small stores including a bakery, a cheese store and a vegetable shop. "Tony, you're the chef, what can we get to make a good meal tonight; something easy that needs little cooking?" Looking at the lettuce, I asked, what do you think of a salad?' "Good idea, let's get all of the things you need here and maybe some kind of meat pie in the bakery, if they have one. If you're confident, we can ask Ted and Jean over for supper. You can be sure that will make Brian happy." The baker had small meat pies that consisted of meat and potatoes. We bought five, and hoped that Ted and Jean would join us.

Arriving back at the campsite with our small shopping bags, we walked right over to Ted and Jean's van. There was no sign of Brian anywhere. "Ted, Will you and Jean join us for dinner tonight? By the way, do you know where Brian is?

Ted said, "He left just after you boys, and said he was going to a bank, and sure we would love to have supper with you."

Jean instantly offers, "I will help, just let me know what you need me to do."

"We need a salad bowl for the greens, and we have bought a meat pie for each of us."

Jean went into their camper and came out with a big clear plastic bowl, and asked, "Will this do for the salad? I have matching small bowls too."

"Marvellous, just warm the pies, and Tony and I will wash the lettuce and prepare the salad."

Jean took the pies and said, "Give me some idea of what time you will need the heated pies. "Do you know when Brian will be returning?"

"We'll make the salad, cover it and give him and hour or so; we will just warm our meals and if he's any later, he will have to eat alone."

"I will be going out again tonight with Lisa, so I will leave shortly after nine o'clock." It was now 6.00, and we were sure Brian would be back in the next hour. Tony and I took the vegetables to the sink the washroom to wash them. As we walked over there, Tony said. "I wonder if they realize why Brian goes to a bank every day; I am sure they would be very interested know how much cash is in his shoulder bag."

"You are right, and we know he goes to as many as he can get into before they close. It's after six, and I would have thought he would be back by now." "Yes, but remember some could be open late, like the ones in Germany where we bought the tent."

When we arrived back at our site with the veggies washed, Jean and Ted said they say Brian walking in Brian walking in. He immediately asked me, "What time do you plan on coming back tomorrow morning, as I assume the car will be here fairly early, and if it is we can leave by midday."

I answered, "I can be back anytime you like, but I will be here at 10.00 am for sure." Tony asked, "Are we going to try and get your transit visas for Hungary, or go right into Yugoslavia?"

"Ted chided in, "Yugoslavia is a great country, and is communist so it is not easy to get into. They will ask a lot of questions at the border. We were there a few years ago. Make sure you get your passports stamped on the way in, as they ask how long you intend to stay."

"We assumed that communist Hungary would be an easier country to get into, provided we got the transit visas." Tony said, "That's great, but the best route for us is through Yugoslavia, because going through Hungary will take us far away from the direction in which we are heading."

"So Brian, you make the decision on which route to take"

"I think the quickest route to Turkey would be the best, but if we have trouble at the Yugoslavian border, and have to go back through Hungary, it will cost us a lot of time. We need to stay here one more day and get a visa for Hungary. If we have to change our route at the Yugoslavian border, we should have our visas in hand or we will be delayed even more."

"This I agree would be sensible, but you better be back in the morning by nine, as we may all have to go to the Hungarian Embassy to get transit visas and other documents."

Jean was very impressed with our salad and had already started to heat up our meat pies. Brian told Tony, "You can make a salad like this anytime you want, and I will buy you bowl like this one. I think salads are a very inexpensive meal and a terrific idea in hot weather, like this."

On returning from completing all the washing up, Jean had made coffee. Ted put a bottle of Brandy on the table, "This will be better than sugar, try a drop of this in your coffee."

'I guess it will be a difficult night for you, Alan saying goodbye to Lisa."

"More than likely, I will see her again, meanwhile, I'll make the most of my time with her as I'll be away from here tomorrow, What do you think Brian?"

"Very true, "I will consider leaving and heading for Yugoslavia, as a very personable young lady at the bank today mentioned that it can sometimes be easier to cross the border into Yugoslavia late at night. I agreed."

I went to freshen up, Tony decided to go and change also.

"From what we discussed earlier, the lady will be here." Brian was very inquisitive and asked what we discussed."

"You will have to ask Alan yourself; as you well know some things we do just like you, we keep to ourselves. Alan is a man of more experience with women than I, and we have developed a friendship of trust and respect. This is what I really like about him. We can talk to each other about our private experiences and we keep them only between each other." Ted agreed with me and admired the wonderful camaraderie we had. It was a terrific thing to have.

Tony changed, and came out wearing long pants and a nice short sleeve shirt. This was the first time I had seen him dressed in anything other than shorts and T-shirt. Tony smiled and said, "I might as well look as smart as I can, if she comes, in case she wants to go out for a drink."

Jean commented, "good for you, a girl will always respects an effort to impress her. Especially knowing you have a very limited wardrobe when travelling with a backpack."

Brian wanted to play cards, but asked if they should bet on which girl turned up first, Alan's or Tony's. Jean said, "Leave the boys alone, let's play cards, what happens should not be our concern. You have done enough betting on this, you guys should sit on the bank by the river, relax and enjoy the alpine scenery."

Brian commented, "You sure you are right, who is dealing and what is the bet tonight. Ted answered "That's more like it now, do you young fellows want to join us or sit on the river bank?"

We both agreed, we were not gamblers, so the river bank would be fine for us to relax by until our dates arrived. We sat there, far enough away from them, so that they couldn't hear us. I told Tony that I heard what he had said about our friendship while I was getting dressed, and I thought it was well put.

Tony said, "I must tell you that I am really nervous about tonight, I hope Sasha turns up alone. I consider those two Scandinavian women are out of my league."

"That is not true Tony; all you have to do is consider my circumstances with Lisa."

"There is no way I would have been connected to a girl from a rich family back home, but as they say, love has no boundaries. Many times you would read of holiday romances, some girls are happy with this, but you have to consider the girl's feelings."

It was eight-thirty, and it looked very much like both women could turn up at the same time. This might prove to be interesting, because we knew what Lisa wanted to do. A double date was not on, as far as she is concerned."

"You may be right Alan, but women can change their minds unexpectedly."

"We should remember there are two of them. I hope they recall I have a date."

"I just hope that Sasha comes alone."

His answer came a minute later, when a voice from behind us said. "It sure is a lovely view from here, and just as nice as I expected." Sasha arrived alone, and she looked stunning. We jumped to our feet and smiled. Tony agreed, "the view is nice but it would be better if there was a bar overlooking the river."

"I know of a nice bar not far, would you like to check it out Tony?"

"Sure I am not well acquainted with pubs in this area."
    "I bid them a nice evening.
    Sasha asked, "what time is your date coming, Alan?"

"I know Lisa finishes work at nine, soon after that".

"You go and have fun; hopefully I will see you again Sasha, before we leave Vienna."

It wasn't long before I heard a car horn and saw Lisa. After I got into her car, she kissed me with a look that any man would love to see. From what she told me earlier in the restaurant, we were to be heading to her parent's house, and probably right to her bedroom.

If we felt like it later on this evening, we might go to the very nice hotel with a small deck and tables right on the lake. We could have a few drinks and talk. It was a hot evening, so it would be beautiful at midnight.

"Wow you have the best ideas, but I must tell you the car will probably be back in the morning; if so, we will leave in the afternoon. That is why we have to make the most of our time together tonight. You will have to drive me back to the campsite by ten.

"That will be okay, but if you do not wake up on time we will be late and I do not intend to set an alarm."

With a very sexy and inviting smile on her face, she said, "You are forgetting one thing lover, you are sleeping with me, and you may not get too much sleep."

As we went up to the bedroom, she said, "I want to have shower, so brush your teeth and get read

After our lovemaking, we got dressed and we drive 15 minutes around the lake into the Danube Valley to this small hotel. It was busy and very popular place. The hotel was extremely close to the lake on beautiful grounds with lovely neatly cut grass and flower beds. It was not a big place; it may have been four floors high and very old. It looked like it was of Alpine architecture. There were many big wooden beams as if in a giant log cabin.

We parked and walked down to the dimly lit deck and were lucky to find a table there. A waiter came out and said, "Hi Lisa, Are your parents not here tonight? and who is this young man you are with?" "Anton, I would like you to meet Alan. "I met him a couple of days ago at work, and my parents are away at the moment. "Very nice to meet you sir, what would you like to drink?" "The lady will have a martini, and I will have a Stella."

"Please bring us a salsa dip with some chips, also." "Well Lisa this seems to be your favourite place. Do you come here with your parents a lot?"

"Yes this is a regular spot for mum and dad, and they often bring me. It is such a lovely place on warm summer nights."

The waiter returned with our drinks and dip. Lisa said, "I always like to have something solid to eat with a drink."

"You're very wise and should not drive for a least an hour after each drink" "That's fine as this place is open really late." She got up and came around behind me, and with her arms around my neck, spoke very low and discreetly in my ear "have you thought any more about staying with me? You know my parents are open-minded and would let you stay with us for a while. We have nice guest room and they would be happy for you to stay in there."

"Our love life would have to be discreet, but I'm sure we would work it out." We looked into each other's eyes, holding hands for a moment; Lisa had a smile that I would never forget, I love you, and that's not something I've been able to say for a long time. I went through a hard break up six months ago, and will be dreaming of holding you in my arms every night while I'm on the road. You waiting for me will prove that we are meant for each other."

We finished our drinks and got up to leave. Lisa left the money on the table and we headed back to her place.

She led me back to the car with a desire in her eyes that only meant one thing, and that was that we would have a night we wouldn't soon forget. When we arrived back at her place, we pulled each other's clothes off, and fell on the bed to make love, and fall asleep in each other's arms.

After waking up about ten the next morning, we washed and dressed, then we got back into her car. Driving back she said, "If Brian gets angry because you are late, you could leave him and stay with me; what do you think?"

I know Brian will be a little upset, however, he needs me for this trip and he will get over it very quickly.

When we arrived at the gate, there was no sign of our car. Lisa looked at me and said, "I should not delay your departure anymore, the car should be here before midday. I will stay with you until it arrives, and if I'm late for work, it will not matter. As we pull up at our site, we saw Brian sitting under Ted and Jean's awning drinking coffee. He remarked, "I have my driver back, but I have no idea what has happened to my passenger."

Lisa and I exited her car then she came over and put her arms around my waist. She told Brian, "You had better look after him because he's really special to me."

"I will not leave until I know that Tony's alright, Brian said; of course, we also need the car back."

Jean offered us coffee and breakfast.

"We never had time for breakfast; Alan woke up late and was so concerned about getting back here as soon as possible, thank you."

Ted asked with a wink, "what did you do to him Lisa; he is always up at the crack of dawn making breakfast and having a shower?"

Jean served us coffee, and asked, "would you like some toast?"

"Sure, Lisa said, that sounds wonderful."

Before we could finish our toast and coffee, there is the sound of a loud horn. Our repaired car was behind the tow truck that was coming towards us. Brian was glad the vehicle was back and before the fellow could lower the car from his truck, he walked over to him and pulled a bundle of cash out of his pocket to pay the man the remainder of the repair bill.

Brian called me over, gave me the keys and told me to go for a drive and let him know how she ran. The man will wait until you come back with a report on how the car handles now. I beckoned Lisa over, saying, "Come on, we'll go for a test drive."

We only drove down the street to the first main intersection; then she directed me around the block and back to the camp site. This was the best it has ever handled; it was never this good, even when we first got the car in England. Lisa commented to me that there was lots of room in the car, and we could have a lot of fun in it.

Back at the camp site I told Brian it was running perfectly, and now we could load her up and she should be fine. Brian thanked the mechanic and he drove off.

Lisa put her arms around my neck, kissed me and started to cry; quietly telling me this was it, for what would seem an eternity; I know you are leaving today. We walk over to the edge of the river and I put my arms around her and held her until she stopped crying. I kissed her and said, "You are in my heart, and we will be together again soon, I promise." She calmed down and said "sorry but I really thought I would not break down on your departure."

"Alan, I would like to leave quickly now. Send me post cards, as many as possible, and please call this phone number." She gave me her parent's home number. If you have a chance any night between 9.30 and 10.00, call. I normally get home by 9.30, and they will take a message if I'm not home. Leave a number, if ever possible where I can call you. I will wait by the phone for your call every night. I will really miss you, and heart is set on meeting you in England soon." She kissed me and rushed off.

As she drove away, a car passed her and stopped right by us; Tony got out. We saw him give Sasha a quick kiss before she left. I cannot wait to have a confidential chat with Tony to find out how his evening was, and what happened.

CHAPTER 22

Brian was glad to finally be able to leave, and yelled out; "Lets pack, we are leaving today."

Tony packed efficiently. He took down my tent before Jean and Ted could get everything out of Brian's. It was not easy to get the heavy boxes of tin food into the back of the trunk. It was very hard to reach, and I carefully sorted everything so that the supplies were at the back as they were the last things we would use.

The last things in were Brian's canvases, easel and art supplies, that we have not yet seen him use. These had to be kept in good order, so he could show customs at any border that he was a travelling artist. Later we would understand why.

Brian said, "I'm confident we will be fine, even when in Turkey."

Ted stated, "Jean and I wish you all a safe journey to Singapore. It's been a lot of fun. We have enjoyed meeting you."

Brian is eager to get going so we all get in the car and drive to the camp office to hand in the washroom key and sign out. Then we take off.

Tony was checking the map for our route out of the city. The main street out of Vienna had a lot of traffic lights, but the traffic wasn't too heavy and we moved quickly along the main road.

The car was riding well with all of us in it; even with the trunk full again it was not as low as it was before. Brian commented, "We're off to a good start, at this rate we should be able to travel at a good speed on the highways, what do think, Alan?"

"Sure, should be fine." I replied with a long sigh.

Brian, as usual wanted to stop at a bank before we went on the highway. "Alan, there is a parking lot up there on the right, pull in."

Tony was aware that the chances of getting into banks in Yugoslavia were not that easy; probably the best probabilities were only in Zagreb and Dubrovnik. The route we took was down the coast and along a rocky ravine which was the border between Yugoslavia and Albania. We then could proceed to Greece. The extremely elevated road between the two communist countries could prove to be very interesting. There were no big towns in this area according to the map, although there were some small settlements along the Adriatic coast.

Brian returned about an hour later. For sure, he went to more than one bank and replenished his funds once again. He had a cold can of cola for each of us and a sandwich. He said that it was a good idea for us to eat now, so we would not have to stop again until supper. That way we might make it to the border before nightfall. It would most certainly appear Brian planned on a very late night crossing of the border, in the hopes it would be a hassle free crossing. We drove all afternoon along on a major road, not a highway which meant we should reach the border late at night for sure.

The scenery was pleasant; some small mountains and rolling hills Most of the time we were on the floor of a valley surrounded by forests. We crossed some lovely rivers and we saw a few small lakes. We were now on a quiet single lane road. It was not a main road, because two trucks could not pass safely. The woods were extremely dense and it was now dark. It was a strange and eerie feeling driving at night on a road with no other traffic or lights. The forest was close to the road, with its tall trees, making it a very sinister drive. There were no road signs, and we were running on deserted roads as per Tony's map reading.

Tony mentioned that according to his map, we should reach the border shortly, and that there was a river ahead. His map reading was correct. It was about eleven when we saw lights ahead. We had made it to the border. The Austrian side was easy; we just showed our passports and crossed over the narrow bridge to the Yugoslavian side.

The border barrier was down. On the other side there was no sign of anyone, so I sounded the horn and a guard with a rifle over his shoulder appeared. He, simply said, "Tourists?" I answered, yes and showed him our passports. He glanced at them looked at us in the car, handed them back and said, right. Then he lifted the barrier and we sailed through. As we passed the guard hut, we saw the other guard asleep in there.

"That was easy, just as I was told, to find a quiet border at night and it would not be a problem," Brian stated.

I drove until one o'clock, before deciding that I needed break for an hour. We safely stopped in a small clearing; it was well off the road.

I must have been very tired, because I did not wake up until four in the morning with a stiff neck. I quietly opened the door and walked around the car. It was dark and damp but very warm. Before I got back into the car, Tony and Brian were awake. Brian was moaning about the damp, and complaining of a stiff neck.

I started the car and put the lights on, after telling them both to walk around the vehicle, stretch, and then we would get back on the road. In less then two hours it would be light, and we should start looking for a place to stop and have coffee. There wasn't any sign of any café or place to buy coffee. Finally, coming out of the quiet forest road and on to more of a highway, we started to see heavy trucks and some light traffic.

Yugoslavia was a poor country. There were places where you saw some old farm-like cottages in poor repair. Most of the people work on the land to earn a living, and their modes of transportation are donkeys, horses and even oxen. The road heading into Zagreb in the north is busy, smooth and in great condition, no pot or shell holes from the recent civil war.

After travelling for quite some time, Brian wanted to stop anywhere that looked like a reasonable place to get a drink. I pulled into a gas station with a small building next to it. There were some tables and chairs outside. We had to fill up with gas, and check out the café.

While the guy filled our fuel tank, Tony went over to the tables. An old woman came out and motioned to him to sit down. Brian paid cash for the gas, and walked over to Tony. We parked right beside the table he was sitting at.

There was only a very basic hand written menu, and not one of us could understand it. There was some English printing, but not enough to make any sense of. The elderly lady came out with an assortment of drinks, (empty bottles and cans) and an astray. She guessed we were tourists, probably by our clothes. We chose some drinks and she disappeared inside to get them; within a short time she then returned with them.

In very poor English she said, "Food you want, eat yes." She wanted us to go inside the back room. She pointed to the small doorway where we could look at the food. We went to see what she had to offer. There were some vegetables with a meat pie. We had no idea what was in it. There were a few cold pies and sandwiches. Brian saw enough, and suggested we have the drinks and move on.

There was no bill; the lady just said five by holding up her hand and counting her fingers. Brian gave her the smallest coin he had which was 10 denara. She bowed to us and smiled, and then she backed away into her kitchen. We deducted from this situation and that it was pretty inexpensive in Yugoslavia.

As we drove off, we pulled away from the main road and into a small town. Brian told me to park the car wherever I could and he would look for a bank. The street is so narrow that two cars the size of ours could not pass. I found a place to park, and Brian wandered off down the high or main street. He seemed extremely satisfied to do this on his own.

We have had a long drive, and decided to lie across the seats and relax for an hour, or however long it took Brian to find a bank.

He wasn't gone very long, and came back happy that he was able to find a one easily.

To leave this small town was really difficult. It was a long and slow drive, as we followed people with hand carts wandering on the road without looking. The locals are not used to seeing many cars or trucks. Quite a few people on the street were looking at our big car. This was an unusual sized vehicle for them.

We were finally clear of the town and back on the main road, and we had only driven for an hour, when we saw a sign for another small town or village. Brian wanted to check it out. Since we lacked eggs, bread and other staples, he suggested this may be the place to get some supplies, and stock up again.

I parked the car in a nice position under a tree to keep it cool. Brian again wants to see if there is anywhere he can get money when we reach Turkey. His main concern was with the expense on the car. He felt he had depleted his budget more than he would have liked.

Tony and I decided to take a walk down one of the very narrow side streets. I have never seen anything like this; it was really unusual, and what you might call ancient. We saw old buildings that looked similar to something you might find in a history book It was like stepping back in time, the street was so narrow that our car could not pass another.

The street was paved with cobblestones that were very uneven, and not very comfortable to walk on. There were no shops or bars, as it appeared to be a residential street. We now know how our grandparents lived. When we were back on the main road, we saw people carrying bags of produce, crossing. We walked down another very narrow way, which was more like a path than a street. This was a busy place with lots of people. About fifty yards down, there was a small clearing, and park like area with tents and canopies.

This was a small farmer's market. As we wandered in, we could see that the vegetables and fruit were fresh. After looking around, we decided to buy six figs, one pound of cherries, 3 lettuces, half a dozen eggs and a large loaf of bread, all for 19 denara which was about $1.20.

Returning to the car with our shopping, we found Brian waiting for us by the car with his arms folded and looking a little upset. His comment was, "why so long, where were you?" Opening the bag and showing him what we bought, we ask him to have a cherry He took some and his mood changed. We told him about our walk and the marketplace. We then got into the car and drove on.

CHAPTER 23

The road out of this village is much easier than the last one, and we were now on the main highway heading into Rijeka Yugoslavia, the gateway to the gulf islands. The scenery ahead was quite spectacular, as we were coming down from an elevated mountainous area.

The City of Rijeka on the northeast coast was ahead and easily visible. This meant we would soon be travelling along the coastal road. It was one of the more popular drives, as the views of the Adriatic Sea are very pleasant. The mountain road was elevated along the rugged coast line, and had many off road places to stop and enjoy the view.

As we approached the port city, we could see a policeman in the middle of the road directing traffic. She stood on a small round concrete platform in the middle of the intersection. She was blowing her whistle and directing very efficiently. This was temporary, as there were no nearby traffic lights working. It was a very busy intersection, and I could see you had to be sure to indicate the direction you were going so the traffic comptroller knew where to direct you. The city road was directly ahead with one fork on the right going to the south, and the other going to the north. Our direction was clear; we headed straight into the city for Brian to collect some more funds.

This was a big city, and banks were easily visible on the main street, I stopped outside one and Brian went in, and came out quickly. We located four more banks. After the last one Brian said, "Let's head for the coast and the next big city; Dubrovnik, which is about 200 miles away. Let's find a nice place on the coast for lunch, and maybe we'll find a beach, and then you can have a swim Alan."

Now, out of the city and heading along the coast, we saw children selling fruit on the side of the road. The road was wet, so there must been a heavy rain storm. We were stopping a lot because of many accidents. Some were serious, with ambulances and fire trucks racing by. It was an eerie situation, as we were travelling in bright sunshine, with steam coming of the motorway.

Brian said, "let's stop and get something from one of those poor children." This was surprising because I thought he would want to get in as much distance as possible. We had not seen him in this mood, ever! As soon as we stopped, two young boys came over to our car with wild strawberries that they would trade for food. I must tell you that I was astonished that they were not looking for money.

Tony offered them a packet of mints, and we got a big smile. They gave us a pound of wild strawberries. This is an extraordinary deal because a pound of strawberries in London would get you 6 packets of mints. English candy in this part of the world was rare; this meant that it was expensive. One of the young boys put the packet into his pocket and never opened them. This would be a huge bartering tool for him later, I'm sure. Survival, not business is their motivation.

We saw some wonderful beaches nearby; which were in quite secluded areas, Brian said, "take the next road, and we will stop for lunch near a beach. Without any hesitation, I turned on to the next road, which was very steep with sharp turns. The street was in perfect condition, so it was enjoyable driving down to a beach in the hot weather.

Brian stated that he was going to make a salad, so if we wanted to go for a quick swim, we should go now. I swiftly changed and was quickly in the water. I swam out a little way, and then turned to swim back, enjoying the amazing view of the rugged coastline that we were driving along. After a short swim in the sea and a salad for lunch, Brian wanted to find a campsite, so in the late afternoon, we started looking for one. Driving up from the beach was an interesting task because this is a steep climb and the car very heavily loaded.

After driving for an hour, we saw a sign for a camp site, we turned left off the highway, and soon reached a really great campsite. When we pulled up in front of the office, Brian went in, and came out quite hastily, jumped in the car and yelled, "Let's go now. I drove out speedily, and he informed us that the man wanted to see his passport. When he showed it to him it, he said, "there's no stamp, how did you get into the country? You must have an entrance date stamped where you come in, with date and time of entry." Now we have a problem Brian said. "Wherever we stop, they will be looking for that stamp."

I suggested we try and look at guest houses, and if we pay cash, we may get a good deal and a peaceful night's rest. Brian asked Tony if he would be alright with this, as it was going to cost more than a campsite. I think we may stand a better chance of getting a place to stay. Tony thought a good night in a bed with breakfast served in the morning would be great. There were lots of signs for bed and breakfasts, we stop at one and had the same problem. We each took turns at going in to each guest house we passed. There were always vacancies and good rates, but they all wanted to see is our entry stamp.

We were driving at a point that was very high above the coast, when we came to a guest house on its own. It was my turn to try, and I was hoping to have some luck. I knocked on the door and a short man with a beard answered.

"Good day, how are you? I am afraid I do not speak your language." Then with a strong English accent, he said, "no problem mate, how many are there of you? I only have two rooms, one single and one double."

"Great, do we have to sign in, and do you need identification?"

He replied, "If you are all English and pay cash, I do not have a problem. I serve a good English breakfast, and you can have an evening meal if you like." I waved to Brian and Tony to come on in and meet our host for the night. He led us upstairs to the rooms.

"I live alone and have a maid coming in to help me cook and clean; my name is Andy, and if you need anything please ask."

Brian said, "Let me pay you now and the boys will go and get the luggage." He pulled a wad of money from his pocket. We knew Brain didn't want us to see how much money he had, or how much he would pay. He did know, however, that it was easy to make a good deal with cash. We left them in the kitchen to make the deal; "you cannot miss the magnificent view out over the water. Andy said, "There will be a cold beer on the table for you both when you return." When we returned the beers where there, just has he promised.

I gave Brian his brown shoulder bag and case. The amazing thing was he walked in leaving the shoulder bag in the car. He quickly and grabbed the shoulder bag and asked me to carry his suitcase up for him. The single room he had was very nice with a fantastic view of the ocean. Our double room was larger, with two lovely single beds, and a big window with an excellent view of the clear blue Adriatic Sea.

The house was long and narrow, so all the windows faced the sea. It was on a slight angle, so Brian's single room at the rear was facing the Adriatic. Unfortunately, at the back, one can't really see clearly both ways along the coast. We headed back down to have our beers and enjoy the magnificent view of the sea.

Andy was interested in where we were heading. When we told him Singapore, he was astounded and asked, "Why so far? I gave him a summary and he remarked that, as soon as one enters Turkey, it will not be so European and touristy. I had been told this by other travellers when I originally came here from England. He told us that Brian had paid for the night.

Andy, "what attracted you to come here from England to live?" He said, "It's a long story, but I met a girl here while on holiday many years ago, and I decided to leave England to be with her. I purchased this place ten years ago, and have loved living here. Unfortunately, it did not work out with her, as she was not interested in running a guest house."

"It's strange how the path of travel leads you, and you never know what will happen. I met a waitress in Wien (Vienna) and we hit it off right away. We were only together for a very short time, but we had a wonderful time together. She asked me to call her whenever I could. How much does it cost to call Austria from here?"

"It is very expensive, but I can let you know, if you would like to call her tonight," replied Andy.

"I will pass, and send her a postcard. I'll write it and leave it for you to post whenever you can," I said. "Alright, I have stamps you can buy and post it on the road when you stop at a gas station".

I told him how Brian, Tony and I got together. I drive, and Tony is our paying passenger. Brian is an artist, although we have yet to see him paint anything. He seemed more intent on travelling at the moment.

"Well I must shortly start supper for you guys" he says as he starts to go.

My interest was in getting to the water, and I ask, "Can we get down to the water from here and is there a nice sandy beach close by."

Andy said, "As you can tell we are very high up here, and there is a beach, but to get to it, you have go out to the main road, turn right and take a narrow dirt road. You will have to walk, as your car is too wide to make the turns safely. Then you follow a very narrow path down, it is very steep and in places there is a sheer drop, so if you do not like heights, don't attempt it."

"Wow, I am the adventurous type, and it sounds like something I want to do for sure; so if we walk, how long will it take?'

"It will take approximately 25 minutes down, and maybe 30 minutes up again. You can assume a one hour round trip to be safe. If you leave now you have plenty of time to get down there, have quick swim and return for supper. I will have dinner ready for seven."

We went up stairs and told Brian of our plans; he was not too thrilled with the idea, as it sounded dangerous. We went anyway.

Making our way along the road was hazardous, as there was no real path. After a few minutes of walking, we reached the dirt track road. This was a very rough way, and the car would not make it down very far as there were two single tracks with lumps in them and some grass growing in the middle all the way. I know that I would not even have attempted to drive near this area with the car. When we reached the point where the track ended, there was just enough room to turn around a very small vehicle.

The path down lay under the shade of some trees, and was quite wide and in very good condition. When you left the shade of the trees, you could see it was a very steep and narrow path. This for sure would be very secluded and remote, if we ever we got to the beach. There was a goat path two feet wide, and in places it was so narrow you had to walk sideways with your back to the cliff. The sheer drop was about 100 feet. It wasn't a path for anyone who was not fit. We now could understand why it was going to take 25 minutes to get down even though it didn't look very far.

The beach was now visible, probably about thirty feet wide and made of pure white sand. As we sat on the beach, we looked up to see the path we came down. We rested for a while in the warm sun; we then headed into the water for a swim. The water is clear but a little cooler than I expect despite hot sun. After swimming for a half hour, we decided we should head back, as the climb up is going to be a lot more arduous and take longer. We want to be back for mealtime.

We heard the sound of a high speed boat approaching, but we couldn't see it; however, it soon passed by us very fast and close to the shore line. The people in the boat waved, and then turned and came back onto the beach.

A young fellow with a lovely looking girl walked up and asked us something in a language we did not understand. The young man shook his head, and couldn't believe that we walked down there. As we started back up the path, we waved goodbye as they stood on the beach impressed that we had made it down, and now are quite casually headed back up.

Arriving back at the house, Andy smiled and asked, "Did you get to the beach?" We replied, "sure did, and wow, the path was very narrow in places."

"It really was a challenge. If you got past that point of heading down, you would be okay, that was why it was secluded and remote." "Most people that get to the beach are locals, and they will only get there by boat. I had no idea you would be so brave, I really thought you would have come back and told me it was too dangerous. You both have a good sense of daring and adventure. Very few people that have stayed here and wanted to go to the beach have ever made it down that path."

"Your friend Brian; has been in his room since you left."

I said, "That is because he is probably asleep. We had a long night yesterday, and crossed the border very late at night. We had problems trying to find a camp site, and then we started trying to find a guest house and finally came to you."

"That was strange because business was not good at the moment, and along the route you came you must have seen plenty of places. Were they all full, or did you come across the border with no stamp?"

"It was the latter, but don't mention that to Brian, as he was very upset when we were refused entrance into a campsite."

"I would suggest, under the circumstances, that I take my car out of the garage and you put yours in it until you leave. It will be a tight fit, but better to be safe. Some of these local people can't be trusted, and they may report your car and registration. Let's arrange that now. I do not want you to have any more problems,."

When we switched the cars, I told Andy, "we have to come up with a good excuse to tell Brian; otherwise he may get upset that we revealed the information to you about the entry stamp situation."

"I will tell Brian that with so much gear in your car; it would be more secure locked in the garage."

"If you are up before him, you can take it out early and he will never know. I have a feeling that you do not get on that well with him. and realize there might be something afoot. He has a lot of cash on him and that's not usual in this part of the world. Europe is quite a safe place, but he should still be careful. In what direction are you aiming, it is not such a good idea to head into what I may term "unforeseen circumstances.""

"Thanks for the advice, Andy. We will contemplate what our plans will be when we get closer to the Turkish border. We'll change for supper and wake Brian, so we can be down for dinner by seven, as you wanted."

Upstairs, we knocked on Brian's door and he grumbled in a half awake voice, "what you want?" "Sorry to wake you Brian, but supper will be ready at 7.00, we'll see you down there okay?" "Sure" was his reply.

When we sat down at the well laid out table, Andy asked if we would like wine or beer with our dinner. "Wine would be great for me" Tony wanted the same. Andy poured the wine, it went well with our chicken dinner, There was still no sign of Brian, so Andy volunteered to go up and ask him if he was coming down to dinner.

The dining room suite was very old; it had beautiful mahogany, carved chairs, oval table, buffet and large china cabinet. The silverware was exquisite, and the glasses went perfectly with the set. This was a layout that would be fit for a show house or a five star hotel.

Brian came down with Andy. When he walked in and saw the table, he stopped and looked for a moment at the beautiful layout. Andy asked him to have seat and enjoy some wine. He would go and get the garlic bread and salad.

"I hope everyone likes a Caesar Salad with their chicken," Andy chimed.

There were no complaints from anyone; this was a total luxury that we never would have imagined having, especially when on a tight budget. The salad and garlic bread were completely finished. Andy was very glad we were enjoying everything, and he said he didn't want to see leftovers from the garlic bread and salad.

He treated his guests just like a restaurant, in that everything was freshly made

Brian seemed extremely unsettled and quiet. This had to be one of the most solemn dinners I ever had. After a very nice apple pie and ice cream desert, Brian headed for bed and Andy offered us a coffee and liquor on the patio. We accepted, and very impressed. When we were finished, we thanked Andy and said goodnight.

We are all down for breakfast at seven, and Andy served us eggs, bacon, mushrooms, and toast. The coffee was excellent, and Brian had his usual pot of tea. On the table were some post cards with views of the beautiful Adriatic coast line. Finishing my breakfast first, I grabbed a post card and started to write to Lisa. Brian was curious and asked who I was sending the card to. "It is for Lisa. I promised that I would send one to her whenever I could". I followed that with one to my parents in Southampton. Finishing both cards, and my journal, Andy came in and said, "If you give me the cards, my housekeeper will post them in Dubrovnik today. I was touched at his kind gesture and thanked him. I asked him how much the stamps would cost, and he answered, "This is my treat. One day, maybe I will have the pleasure of meeting you again with Lisa."

Soon we were all in the car, waving goodbye to Andy and his great hospitality. This was a place I would love to return to sometime in the future with Lisa.

CHAPTER 24

The road into Dubrovnik was busy in the mid-afternoon, but traffic was moving extremely well. This maritime village was ringed by a thick medieval wall with majestic stone embankments enclosing the harbour. The scenery was absolutely spectacular; it had many elevated views of the Adriatic Sea and the coastline make for an interesting drive.

Passing through Dubrovnik with its cobbled streets and narrow back alleys was fairly easy; we then headed along a ravine with a serious drop to a river. This road was very dusty and deserted. There was no traffic as we climbed up the side of a watery ravine. Looking down into the ravine, I saw trucks, cars and a burnt out bus. This was the border to Albania; there were huge shell holes in the road. This was evidence of some heavy shelling and fighting here.

This main road was very quiet, and we still did not see any traffic. The barriers around the holes made me think this was not a particularly safe route to be taking, yet it was the best way to get to the Greek border. We hoped we could cover a good amount of distance, in as little time as possible. When we turned the corner, it looked like we had to turn back as the bridge ahead had some very large shell holes in it, but there was no alternative route. The wooden barriers were basic and easy to move, but marked an extremely dangerous area for pedestrians. We put them back for this reason.

Brian was disappointed, and wanted to see if there was any way I could drive through. Walking out to the holes, which were about or 2 feet in diameter, we saw there was just enough room to drive between them. It would be very tight because some tire marks showed a very small car had made it. Since ours was so much wider and had a long wheel base, it would be tight. The only way I could attempt this was for Tony to walk backwards in front of me and guide me. But first I had to measure our wheel tracks and base to see if it was possible. It was, barely.

Brian wanted me to go for it, so he walked across with Tony guiding me, I drive very slowly, as I had to drive right over some of the holes. After fifteen minutes of backing and turning inch by inch, we finally got through. Brian cheered at both for doing such an amazing job. He realized that crossing this bridge has cut a day off our journey.

As we passed through the tunnel ahead, we came across some local people with a hand cart. The astounded look on their faces as we passed them was unbelievable. We were sure they wondered how those foreigners had managed to get across the bridge. I now know that the tracks around the holes in the bridge were made with a hand cart, not a car. This makes our achievement even more impressive.

Tony reckons that according to the map, we are about 75 miles from an intersection where we turn right on to a main road and then head for the Greek border. It must be correct, as this is the only other turn off.

We passed through more tunnels and over many more bridges with shell holes in them, it was now late afternoon with no sign of civilisation or campsites. There was nothing but mountains to our left, and a ravine to our right. We didn't see an area big or flat enough to pitch a tent,. Our isolated road trip couldn't end soon enough for us, as we were all very hot and uncomfortable in the mid afternoon heat. My only concern at that moment was to get through to the end of this road. We made it through the area and saw no other traffic.

As we turned a corner, we faced a steep rough uphill climb; the main road ahead had another barrier in front of us. There were piles of rocks with one small opening, and a wooden pole across it. Tony and I got out and removed it, and then we moved some rocks to make the opening wide enough for the car to pass through. We replaced the barriers. If anyone saw us they might have reported us to the authorities. Later we learned that Brian especially, could not take that chance of arrest etc.

The road towards the border was now a pleasure to travel. It was smooth, and the traffic was moving at a steady speed. We were again on a very elevated portion, and we were climbing very slowly on the last part of the ravine road. We will be going downhill as we head for the coast and Greek border. The odd house and small villages make for a more interesting drive. Brian, as usual, wants to go into a town for a bank.

Tony and Brian were sure we could make the border that night, but it might be very late, Brian said he would pay for a motel in Greece, which would be a lot better than the hotels here.

This meant that I would have to speed up a bit more, whenever possible.

The next problem was that we needed to fill up with gas, so at the first station I came to; I pulled in to top up. The young pump attendant came out and was very interested in our car; He spoke only a little English. As soon as he filled the tank, Brian had the cash ready. When we asked how far it was to the border, the man said about 4 hours. That meant it would be dark and about 10.00.

"You can save an hour, let me show you on your map" he said so Tony got of the car and the young man pointed out some other route which was a little off the main road. It meant that the roads were quiet and fast, as there was little traffic, and definitely no trucks. The young man liked to travel fast, and he drove on these roads all the time at very high speeds on his motorcycle.

The street ahead was busy, and Tony suggested, "We are going to make quite a few turns on to what looks like very narrow lanes, but I think these roads will be faster, as they have fewer intersections.

We turned off the main intersection, and were now on a road that looked like it is about a mile of straight driving; I put my foot down and cruised at 80 mph whenever I could. This was the fastest we had ever travelled since starting out from France. Now it was nine o'clock, and we were back on the main road, the border was a couple of miles away.

Our next problem was going to be, how and where we came into Yugoslavia. Without the entrance stamp, this is going to be really difficult for us in finding a campsite. Brian was worried, and wondered what would be our best alibi to safely get over the border. Tony and I agreed that the truth is the best way to go, so we gave the details of exactly where we crossed and played total innocence. This way, if we are separated and interviewed all our stories will be the same. There were two guards, one was asleep and one woke up when we sounded our horn. After he looked at our passports, he sent us through. After we passed, we saw the other guard still asleep.

Brian was anxious, and we had to persuade him to relax and feign innocence. Our story was we were on holiday had no idea about stamps at borders; coming across Europe from England.

As we approached the border check point, it was very busy. I figured that could be to our advantage. They only had four booths and one hold up would cause a traffic jam, which at night would get people upset. The lineup was amazing considering how late it was, and there were only two booths open. After 15 minutes in the lineup it was our turn.

I handed the official our passports, and after studying mine, he looked at me he asked, "How long have you been in the country? I answered two days; He looked at Tony and Brian's passports and said, "Wait here. He picked up the phone, and soon another officer came over to our car and asked us to pull through and park to the right in front of the big building we were all escorted into an office with several other officers, one having a badge with a Union Jack (English speaking) so he would be talking to us.

Just as I expected, we were going to be interviewed one at a time. They asked me in first, the questions were just as I expected; "how did you get into the country without a stamp? And where did you stay?" The one part of our story that I did not collaborate was where we stayed, and of course, how we managed to stay somewhere without an entrance stamp.

I told him of how we wanted to pay cash at a guest house and the guy never asks about the stamp. We had travelled all across Europe and never had a stamp anywhere. He was amused at the fact that the guards were asleep, and we had transited without this stamp. He seems to know of this border crossing and it appeared we weren't the only ones to cross there with the same result.

"Where are all of you heading?" "We are going to Singapore sir", I replied. He was completely taken back with our answer, and, "Sorry about the inconvenience, but we have to check all these things out as some people are trafficking things at night, we will check your car and you can be on your way."

I opened the trunk and started taking out the painting equipment and camping gear, I also showed him all the tin food in boxes. He was quite astounded at the amount of food and said, "thank you for your co-operation, and have a nice trip."

After reloading all the items in the trunk, we headed for the Greek border point and its booth. It should be easy from now on, as we have no bad reports about Greece. Approaching the traffic kiosk and joining the lineup, it was as I expected, the vehicles were going through very quickly. I got to the gate and handed the official our passports; he looked in the car, took a good look at the passports, then asked why we had to go to the immigration office on the Yugoslavian side.

I explained that we came in without getting an entrance stamp on our passports, and now the other officials are satisfied. With that he stamped our passports, smiled and told us to enjoy our stay in Greece. We have now crossed over from a poor communist country to a richer democratic nation with minimal trouble. We breathed a long sigh of relief.

CHAPTER 25

As we drove into the night we were all tired and needed to find a motel. Brian wanted to pull in to the first one we came to. After driving for another hour, we saw a well illuminated motel and pulled in. Brian got out of the car and went to the reception hoping to get a couple of rooms for the night.

The parking lot was paved with rough gravel and I had to drive very slowly hoping not to hit bottom. Tony was a little concerned, as Brian had gone in alone with his shoulder bag. Opening that bag in there with that much cash could be a problem.

We need not to have had to worry; Brian came out with two keys and asked me to drive around to room numbers 107 and 108. This one storey place was just three straight rows of rooms; you just drove up to your room and parked outside it. Brian was glad, he told us this had to be the cheapest hotel he had ever booked into. He told Tony to pay for the next tank of gas and he would call it even.

There was a restaurant in the reception area, and we could have breakfast any time after 7.00 am. We decided to be up for breakfast at 7.30, and Brian would rely on us to wake him in the morning. We guessed he didn't have an alarm clock.

Tony and I were amazed at how nice the rooms were. They were very basic, but clean with a very small toilet and shower. It did not take very long for us to get settled for the night. Tony asked me "how do you feel about going into Turkey with him?"

My answer was simple, "not happy, as this was a country I would not be comfortable travelling through, when you have to consider how much cash he is carrying, and to keep a constant eye on him. This is not something I want to do. He seemed to be very confident that he would not get bothered, and I notice he does not open the shoulder bag anywhere we can see him. He now always has a wad of notes in his pocket."

"Well Alan, I gather that at some stage before the Turkish Border, you will have to tell him that you are going no further with him."

"I have to consider how to get back home and how much money he will pay me. Having only a small suitcase is not the ideal thing to travel with on the road. I will need a backpack."

"Not a problem, Alan I have money, and can loan you some to travel back. We make a great team. I would suggest we wait until we are at a campsite, hopefully one before the Turkish border."

A noisy truck at six in the morning woke up both Tony and I. It really didn't matter, as we had to wake Brian soon. We had to be down for breakfast at seven-thirty as Brian requested. I quickly took a shower, knowing it would take Brian about an hour to get up and be ready from the time I woke him. I banged on his door, but there was no answer. I went back and told Tony who suggested we use the phone, as the call from room to room should be free.

Calling his room seemed to work, but there was still no answer. I left it ringing and went to his door, I heard the phone ringing. After ringing for five minutes, he finally picked it up. He just shouted what the hell do we want, I replied that I was sorry to wake him, but he wanted to have breakfast at 7.30. He did not reply, but hung up. This impoliteness angered me.

"Well Tony, this is definitely going to be the last straw. I will now tell him at the first opportunity, probably, at a campsite before Turkey, that I am definitely not going with with him. You can imagine with this kind of attitude and being so rude to me, the first thing in the morning when we woke him as he requested, there is no way I can handle any more of this type of behaviour."

Tony calmly says, "Let's go for breakfast and wait and see what his reaction will be. I'm sure he will apologize and if not, we should stay calm and wait for the opportunity to deliver the final blow."

We sat in the restaurant having a coffee at 7.30 with no sign of Brian. It was very quiet, as there were no other people around. The breakfast was simple: toast, cereal and a serve yourself buffet. Our meals were fine and the coffee has just been made, so was hot and fresh, just as we liked it. I got a tea for Brian, hoping he will soon be walking in and that this might help his mood.

Ten minutes passed so we get some more cereal and toast. As we sat down, Brian arrived, not looking happy. He sat down, sipped his tea, and complained it was too strong and cold. I was just about to say something to him when Tony nudged me with his foot from under the table. So I asked Brian if I could get him another tea. He grumbled "sure, and a piece of toast would be nice." I ask Tony to get the tea while I got his toast.

As Tony was getting the toast, he told me to stay cool and let him have his breakfast; perhaps he will calm down and relax. He was sure to tell us his problem and explain his rudeness once he had his tea and toast.

At the table all is quiet and we have our breakfast in silence. Brian asked how we slept. We both agreed that we slept very well. Brian said there was a lot of arguing and shouting outside his door at two in the morning which kept him awake.

I looked at him sternly and said, "Was that why you were rude and abrupt when you picked up the phone?" He quietly mumbled that he was sorry about that; he was not in a good mood when we woke him up.

My frame of mind wasn't great and I told him to smarten up or he would be looking for another driver. Tony was startled, as he did not expect me to hit him with a comment like that. This was a result of having lived in close quarters for over a month.

In a totally different frame of mind, Brian apologized for his grumpiness and promised that it would not happen again. "You are right, let's enjoy our breakfast. I will make it up to you by stopping somewhere nice for lunch today, is that fair enough?"

"That sounds reasonable," we said. We got him to change his behaviour quickly and get a bonus. This is an unexpected treat as we thought he had limited funds.

"We need to find a bank today, and get gas coupons here, as there is some kind of shortage of gas. I read about this in the office."

He seemed to be a lot calmer now, as we headed back to our rooms to grab our belongings. We left on our next leg of the journey on the long road through Greece to the Turkish border.

CHAPTER 26

Heavy traffic made moving slow. This was not a good start to the day's travel plans. The target was to reach or get very close to the border before dark. After covering about 60 miles in two hours, the prospect of stopping soon for lunch as Brian promised is not looking good. Brian asked Tony to study the map and see if there was an alternative route that may be quicker. There were no main roads in our direction without going north or south a long way. We decided to stay on this route and hoped the situation improved soon. With that analysis, Brian wanted to head into a town, even if it meant going off our planned route.

Tony told him that there was a large town on the Vardar River in the mountains ahead called Skopje, about 30 miles from where we were. It would most certainly have large banks and maybe we could have lunch there. I found a campsite in a nearby place called Kavalla, which was about 160 miles ahead. The traffic may move quicker, but even at our current pace, provided we leave Skopje by mid afternoon, we should make it well before dark.

Brian was not too pleased and suggested that we have a quick lunch as he needed to get to a bank. We had to get gas coupons as well so we could fill up again. Because the traffic was moving well, we figured we should be in Skopje, Bulgaria (modern day Macedonia) within an hour or so.

Driving into the town wasn't easy. As soon as we got on to the high street, we saw a couple of banks, and Brian immediately asked to stop at the first one. Parking there was easy; the lot was right off the main street behind some big buildings. I parked under a tree in a nice spot that would allow the car to be sheltered from the afternoon sun.

As Brian started to leave the car, he told us to wait there as he would be back soon. I told him we were going to walk with him down the street and find somewhere to get a cold drink, and maybe something to eat. Childishly, and not in a good mood, he replies, "No, I do not need an escort and will be alright on my own."

We walked ahead of him, and we soon saw a sign for a café and turned to tell him that was where we were going, and we would wait there for him.

"I don't understand why you are so demanding today", he said.

I reminded him, "You promised to pay for our lunch after your abrupt and rude behaviour this morning. We are holding you to that."

After a brief moment, he pulled out a bundle of cash from his pocket and gave me some money.

We strolled up to the café. It looked very nice so we went straight in. We saw through the window that just in front of us there were several banks not far apart. For sure, he would wander down as far as he could and go into all the banks possible. This would mean he might be a couple of hours, and we would not see him in the cafe. We had told him to eat wherever he could in the area, when he finished his banking. We would be in the cafe for about an hour or so, if he wanted to eat with us, or else he could meet us at the car. The cafe was extremely clean. There were small booths with flowers between them, and a few tables in the middle which were separated by some very pretty and large plants in earthenware pots. The aroma of some kind of meat sauce and vegetables was in the air. This was truly a pleasant atmosphere, the waitress told us to sit where ever we liked.

We made ourselves comfortable in a nice booth. The waitress gave us menus and asked us what we would like to drink. We figured our server was probably from England, as she had the accent. She smiled, but not like Lisa, just a short pleasant one. We told her ginger ale will be fine, asked what the aroma was coming from the kitchen. I asked her what she recommended we order from the menu.

"What you can smell is a meat stew, this is a typical Greek meal and if you are hungry, you will enjoy this. "That sounds great, but can you tell me does it have and parsnip in it. I cannot tolerate that particular vegetable." It basically consists of lamb, potatoes, carrots and some beans."

Tony immediately said, "Let's have that Alan, it sounds great. We were wondering what part of England are you from." She smiled and said, "Leeds" and asked, where are you from and where are you heading?." "We are from Southampton and are on route to Singapore."

The girl was not surprised and asked, "Are we flying from Athens? "No replied Tony, "we are driving all the way to Singapore." She looked at us, totally amazed at us and said, "You have to be joking

160

right." No it's true, why are you so surprised, it's a long journey, but not impossible."

"The reason I'm surprised is I have been told the route goes through the Middle East, and we have heard recently of several vehicles over there were hijacked or stolen with the occupants killed or left on the road. Their belongings were sold on the Black Market; it has become an accepted way of life."

Tony and I looked at each other and told her that she had just convinced us not to go into Turkey, and thanked her for the information. She left to get our order. Tony expressed to me that with this information, he for sure had no intention of entering Turkey. My opinion was the same; we had to make plans for our route home, after we let Brian know we are not going any further and why.

We would like to relax and visit a few Greek islands before heading back home to England. Tony and I decided the best way to approach Brian was with the factual stories about hijackings of cars on the road beyond Turkey, and we do want to go into such a dangerous situation.

Before our meal arrived, another waitress by the name of Jane came to our table. She was also from England.

She was talking to us for a few minutes and one of the things she told us was that had a bad experience with an English fellow a while ago, and she had been very weary of English men ever since.

Our food arrived and the waitress just smiled and said, "Enjoy your meal and is there anything more you need? We replied, "No thank you, we are fine." The meal was excellent, and we both enjoyed it very much. After having a couple of drinks, an hour had passed and we decided to walk down the street in the direction of the banks and perhaps see Brian.

After passing three banks and walking a quite some distance in the hot afternoon sun, we decided we must head back to the car and wait for him there. Later in the afternoon the car was well shaded from the sun. Reaching the vehicle, I was correct, it was in complete shade. We had to open all the windows and doors, in order for it to cool down. We made ourselves comfortable and sat under the shade of the tree, and we waited for Brian.

Late in the afternoon Brian came walking slowly in, and asked if we would like to go for a drink before we leave. He was in a better frame of mind again. This was due; I am sure to the fact he got to visit a few more banks with complete success in accumulating some more funds.

We thought that was a great idea, and went back to the café where we had eaten. We asked Brian what he had eaten for lunch, he replied, nothing just a bottle of water. We told him of our meal in the café, and to make him happy, I gave him the change from what he had given me. He was impressed, saying that sounds like a very good deal for the price.

The waitress is surprised to see us, and we asked if they had the vegetable stew still available. She replied, "Sure, I will get you a dish right away, and what would you all like to drink?" Brian had a repeat of the lunch we had.

It did not take Brian long to clear his plate, finish his drink and announce that we should be at the Turkish border tonight. He pulled out his cash and asked for the bill; he put money on the table and we left.

My concern was the gas, as we had less than half a tank, so I told Brian we must fill up whenever we get a chance. He tried to think of an excuse, so he could hold onto the coupons he had.

We stopped at a filling station and filled up the car. Tony suggested we fill up in Greece at Kavalla, because you never know what the case will be in Turkey for gas. This worked well and Brian said, "you're right, I will keep the coupons we have, and sell the extras at Kavalla, I'm sure someone there will buy them from us." This was a great comment from Tony, as we knew that we would have enough coupons to fill up with gas, at least to Athens.

Kavalla was now only seventy miles away. This palm fronted Aegean port and ferry hub had several good sandy beaches. Once at the campsite, about 1.5 miles west of the town, we would register and settle down for the night. We planned on breaking the news to Brian soon. Tony found this campsite, and it was on the beach.

When back on the road heading for Kavalla, Brian showed us the gas coupons and said, "The reason I was so long was that I had to line up forever to get these coupons."

He went on to say that you can get so many at each bank. "I had to explain why I needed more than most. I told them I was passing through, and my car was burning a lot of gas. Each bank allows a certain amount of coupons to each customer. You can get the same amount at each bank, as there is no way they know what you have already collected."

The next one and a half hours passed quickly, and we pulled into the campsite. It was a large well spread out spot right on the beach. It was very well organized with gravel roads leading to the sites, and posts at each area where can pitch your tent and park.

We parked outside the office and Brian went in to pay. When he came out, he told us that it was very expensive, and he wanted to find a cheaper campsite.

"Well Brian, "said Tony" I will stay here, as I do not want to go to Turkey with you."

His reaction to Tony was, 'fine, get out of here, and enjoy yourself." He came across fairly calm, but he really was angry. We could tell he was by he was talking. I told him he could look for another driver, as this was the end of the road for me, also. He was seething, and we are all out of the car when he banged his fist on the hood and asked, "What the hell do you mean, Alan?

I walked up to him, grabbed his shirt collar with my left hand, while making a fist with my right, and I asked him if he wanted to argue with me. He was shaking and saying no, but why? I said that I was very clear and had no desire to risk my life trying to keep him and his funds in that shoulder bag safe under the dangerous conditions that laid ahead. Tony yelled "take it easy, Alan let him go." I told Brian to go in and book a spot right here. He was now very nervous, and clearly very worried that I might do something to physically hurt him.

Tony, who was between us, said to Brian, "Let's go into the office. Alan, stay with the car, and we will be back." Tony walked into the office behind Brian; he turned with a big smile on his face and gave me the thumbs up sign. He knew that Brian wouldn't push me anymore, and was wondering what his next move might be to calm down the man who he trusted to take care of him.

I waited by the car, as Brian came out. He came over to me saying "I have paid for a spot here, now how much do you want to drive me to Singapore?" I guess he did not believe us. My response very firm, "nothing; I do not want to go into Turkey or the Middle East as we have been told of some serious hijackings."

He was now very reasonable and asked if we could set up for the night and discuss the options for him later, after dinner. Tony was right behind him giving me the two thumbs up sign for my courage in the showdown.

Setting up our tents did not take long; Tony suggested making a spaghetti dinner. He needed a can of meat plus a can of tomatoes. One of Brian's favourite meals was pasta, so he was absolutely thrilled.

He said, "now that we have a nice spot on the beach, let's get set up and you can go for a swim." He wanted me to cool off and relax. He may have thought I would change my mind and continue with him. Tony was standing behind him and grinning and was glad for this current turn of events. He did not have to fear for his safety.

I checked all the tins in the trunk of the car, as I was sure we still had tomatoes and a can of meat. I found everything; I got a pot of water and set up the stoves. Considering the limited resources he had to work with, Tony made a super meal for us. We used one of the folding tables, so we could eat our meal, and then we set the food on the car hood.

Brian decided that we should sell everything we have left at this campsite. I suggested he ask at the office for a couple of tables so we could spread everything on them and put up some 'for sale signs.' He knew we were serious, and had decided to part ways. Tony and I would go on together.

This was an extremely large campground; I figured there must be more than a hundred people. The office loaned us two folding tables, and the manager brought some wide tape. I found some white cardboard and made some for sale signs. My suggestion was to make up a sandwich board advertising our used camping supplies. This proved to be a very successful idea, as people came from everywhere. Quite a few people who lived nearby in the town also came seeking bargains. Word was out and many items were being sold at an astounding rate. Brian didn't argue with any reasonable priced offer. To our surprise, all of the paintings, canvases easel, pallet and paints which were in pristine condition went too. Even the tents and air beds were sold, on the condition that they would be picked up the next morning.

When all was sold, we took the tables back to the office, and Brian gave the gentleman there a little extra cash for being so helpful. We divided the proceeds and I got a good amount. Brian's plan was simple, go to Athens and sell the car, then fly to Tehran, Iran to meet his friend. He would pay me the bulk after selling the car.

My only concern was travelling with just a suitcase; I really needed a backpack. Brian said he would buy me one in Athens, and pay me then, also. His only request was for us to sell the car for as much as we could, and then get him to the Athens airport. He was going to fly to Tehran; we didn't question his plans, as we just wanted to be as friendly and helpful as we could until we parted company.

I knew very well that selling such a big car would not be easy. It was extremely hard on gas. I told him the more coupons we collected, the more it would help with selling the car. I advised him to go to the banks in Athens and get as many coupons as he could. That would be a great tool to bargain with.

We would also need a lawyer to help with the ownership and registration transfers, since the car was registered in my name.

With limited camping equipment and few sleeping set ups left, we had very little to cook or cook on; our evening meal had to be in a restaurant.

The only supplies we had were some cereal, eggs, coffee and tea bags. We had to look for a store to buy some fresh bread, so we could have breakfast at the campsite in the morning. We did not sell our water bottles, as we needed them in order to survive in this hot, humid weather. This would be our last evening meal together. Brian would have to be in a good mood, or he would be left with a car he couldn't sell.

As we walked out of the camp site to the street, Brian wanted to go in to the first restaurant or café he saw. It had to be close by since it was so hot out, and he was unable to walk very far.

The first presentable place we came to was a family restaurant, which had a menu showing some reasonably priced dishes. The menu was basic, some fish, chicken and some Greek lamb. The décor was typical of Greek restaurants; however. Brian was not impressed by the smell of the food. We convinced Brian to stay at this restaurant, because the dishes looked good, and the prices were in our range.

From the small bar, Tony and I ordered Stella beers, while Brain ordered an ice cola. There were no complaints from Brian, so we were sure he was not going to argue over the last bill for an evening meal. He needed us to help him in Athens, and would rather part on a friendly basis. Looking at the menu, Brian asked us what we would like to have, and what the fish dishes were like in Greece, as we seemed familiar with the menu. We ordered, and the food was delicious. We exited an hour later feeling well fed and full. When we got back to the campground, we retired for the evening.

CHAPTER 27

I was up about six the next morning, as it was really hot and hard to sleep. It was about 30 Celsius, so I decided to go for an early morning swim to cool off. The water felt warm but the air was cooler at this time of the morning. I swam out along the beach for about an hour, and then decided to walk back along the beach. It was quiet, as nobody else was up yet. The distance I swam was deceiving, as it was a longer walk back than I thought.

When I got back Tony was up, and told me he awoke just after me, and saw me swim parallel with the beach. He couldn't believe how far I swam. I told him I was very comfortable swimming in the calm water, and that I have swum so many times in the English Channel back home in Southampton.

When we arrived back at the tents, we had peanut butter on bread and coffee for breakfast. We did not have much food, or many utensils to cook with. Soon, the people who purchased the tents and air beds would be coming to pick them up. Brian had told them to come after 8.00 in the morning. There was no sign of movement anywhere on the site, so I would assume nobody gets up early here.

With plans to get to Athens today, we had to start out at a reasonable time, as the Greek capital was at least a full day's drive away. I knew that Brian would be eager to sell the car, although I think that it will be a difficult task. There are not many American cars in this part of the world, since they are heavy on gas, which is expensive.

It was 8.00 and Brian had still not gotten up, so we decided we would have to wake him. Tony suggested starting the car and sounding the horn, as that noise might move him. We did that.

Ten minutes later he came out and asked what we were doing for breakfast. Tony told him we had one only stove, and he would make him a cup of tea, there was some bread and peanut butter available also. He seemed to be in a good mood, and was really appreciative of the meagre breakfast. I suggested that we take down the tents and have them ready for the people to pick up. Brian agreed, he just wanted to take his few items out of his tent. Our tents were empty, and my case was packed; Tony was also ready to go. Seeing as we didn't have anything to pack in the car, we could leave as soon as the people picked up the all the items that were sold.

There was lots of movement on the site now, and the people came and took everything that they had purchased away. Brian had to still do some last minute bartering. The people knew he was leaving, and were trying to get him to drop the prices even more. He refused, as the prices were very low anyway. Only one customer argued over the price for the tents; Brian told me to put them in the trunk and we would sell them in Athens. That was enough for the guy to quickly change his mind, and hand over the cash amount that Brian had asked for the previous night.

It was extremely hot when we left the site at 8.45. Having sold everything in the car, it became so light that it was riding much higher. It would be a pleasure to drive to Athens; we just hoped the roads were clear and straight. The morning traffic out of Kavalla was very light. Brian asked Tony what the next big town was, and where he could do some more banking. He said that Thessalonica will be on our route, and banks should be open by the time we reach there.

The temperature in the car is becoming almost unbearable, probably close to 34c when we stopped moving. Since we had no air conditioning, we always had the windows open, and when we moved at a good speed, it was not too bad. Stopping at a traffic light was like instant torture, the heat built up quickly. We had lots of bottled water in the car, but it got warm in the afternoon; we still drank the water to keep hydrated. It would have been nice if we could have stopped for a cool drink.

Driving into Thessalonica was a real hardship, as its streets were very old and narrow. Crawling along at a snail's pace on what seemed like the main street, we didn't see any banks. We got the attention of the young man on a bicycle next to our car and we asked him if there were any banks in town. The fellow told us that there was, and it was two streets to the left of where we were.

We turned down a street that was so narrow, our car took up the whole width of the road; we now had no place to turn around. We drove slowly down the winding street, and we came to a bank with a small parking area. This space allowed just enough room for a small car to past.

We knew for sure it was going to be a long wait, because there was a stream of people going in and out of this very small establishment.

There was a line up for more gas coupons and, Brian as a tourist, had no trouble.

This street was not too busy, so our car really stood out to most of the passersby. It was very clear that this was an unusual looking car to them. The sign at the beginning of the lane we were now entering read, narrow lane, no exit. The young man who directed us down here did not mention the fact that one should walk down the lane, as it was too narrow, and came to a dead end.

I got out and looked at the width of the road, and the length of the car, and I suggested to Tony that he guide me so I could turn the car around. Shunting back and forth many times with the car just inches from the wall proved to be a very difficult task. A crowd gathered to watch in disbelief, what we attempting to do. After jolting very slowly for about ten minutes, with the front of the car at one point only two inches from a shop door, we turned the car around. The crowd cheered at our achievement.

It had been almost an hour since Brian went into the bank, so Tony headed in to check out what was happening. Returning, he told me Brian was in the front of the line up for gas coupons, and that the place was a lot bigger than it looked from the outside. The building went back a long way and there was another entrance on the other side. He saw that there was only one person issuing the gas coupons; however, Brian was pretty close to the front of the line.

Brian came out and was surprised to see the car turned around, but I did not comment on the difficulty.

Getting out of Kavalla became a real problem. There was very heavy traffic and the roads were not very wide. It would take quite some time to get to the highway. After what seemed like an eternity, we reached the main road and started moving well.

We wanted to keep going, but Brian saw a hitchhiker and told me to stop. Wow what a shock, you'd never imagine that Brian would want to stop and pick up a hiker. He was a young Swedish fellow, who spoke perfect English and was only going to the next town. I was not sure of the name of it, but we told him we were going that way. He then told us how hard it was getting rides; Brian asked him if he could drive, and if he was adventurous. The reason was now clear why he picked up the man. He was still trying to find another driver to complete his trip. The fellow was not interested, and when we reached his stop, he left us.

Brian decided he wanted to drive for a while. With his poor eyesight, this wasn't a good idea. Brian said the highway was quiet and the road was straight so he wanted to drive for an hour or so. Reluctantly, we let him drive for a while; I felt tired anyway, so I lay down in the back seat and tried to get a little sleep. I awoke quickly when he stopped very suddenly.

Brian wanted to get a beverage, and Tony had decided that he had driven enough. He was wandering on the road, and travelling close to 70 miles an hour, this was not at all safe, and especially with his limited vision. Tony asked me to please take over. Brian did not argue with him. We were cruising at 75 miles an hour with no traffic along a straight and very smooth road; the car was running absolutely perfect. With a limited amount of camping equipment now, we would have to use Tony's fly sheet as a second tent for sleeping.

We approached Athens, the Greek capital and "cradle of modern civilization," we were looking for a campsite. We found one with a view of the Acropolis, Coliseum and Parthenon, that was also close to the island ferries. This campsite had all the facilities one wanted, even a swimming pool and a large office building with a store. It was probably expensive, but it was well worth getting a good sleep and a meal in a posh restaurant.

Setting up was easy and did not take long. Tony remained at the campsite while Brian and I headed into the town to try and sell the car which was registered in my name. There was quite a bit of work involved in selling the car, mainly the ownership transfer. Many garages that I drove into were used car dealerships. All eyes were on us, as it was a rather unusual vehicle that we were driving compared to the small cars Athens.

We finally got some luck; a gentleman was interested. He was very familiar with the vehicle registration office, and could speed up the transfer process. The next part was to receive a reasonable price. My plan was to offer the petrol coupons first as we had quite a few. The man was amazed at how many we had and wanted to buy them à right away. When we told him they were free with the car, he was most certainly ready to make a deal. Setting a price for the car did not take long, as Brian was not interested in bartering too much. His plans were simple, as he wanted to get to the airport as soon as he could.

The registration office we needed to go to was closed, so we had to return in the morning, we asked if he could help us with the transfer of the vehicle registration. He agreed, and we left for our campsite to spend the night, and return in the morning to finish the transactions.

CHAPTER 28

This campsite was very nice and had a good sized swimming pool. Brian was in a good mood, as he was sure the deal with the car would be sorted out soon. He would be able to book his flight and leave. We suggested finding a reasonable place to have a meal. It was getting very late and we were hungry.

We suggested that we try a restaurant just outside the campsite, in order to avoid a parking problem. He was satisfied with our suggestion so we walked out of the campsite, hoping to find a well-priced and air cooled restaurant.

We arrived at the first family restaurant we came to, about fifty meters from the campsite. We studied the menu on the door, liked we saw, and went in. It was extremely clean, and had brightly painted yellow and blue walls, with white chairs and plain white plastic table cloths. This was a typical family style restaurant.

The aroma from the kitchen made Brian curious about what they were cooking. A waiter came over and handed us the menus. Brian was not sure what to have and asked for some suggestions.

We knew their meat stews were excellent, and decided to have the lamb stew. Brian liked the idea, and told us to order whatever we wanted to drink. He would have a melon juice. We asked the waiter for three lamb stews, two Stella's and a cold melon juice.

The meal was wonderful; Brian especially enjoyed it, as he had not had anything like this before. Brian confessed that he knew someone in Tehran, and that was one of the places we would have probably stayed when we passed through. That was why he wanted to fly out there and maybe continue his adventure.

I'm hoping that I will not have too much of a problem with getting Brian to purchase a backpack and a few supplies for me.

"Have another beer guys, this is our last night; I will not be spending any more money on you, this is it, enjoy yourselves," We never had more than one beer at Brian's expense. We now had to walk back to our site, and we were feeling no pain. I knew I'd sleep well, as beer is like a sleeping pill to me.

The walk back was really uncomfortable, as it was terribly hot and humid. It had to be the worst night yet, although it was a common thing in summer here in Greece. Due to the extreme heat, Tony and I decided to go and buy some cold drinks from the camp store which was still open. Brian was agreeable, and gave us some money. He said he was going right to bed in his sleeping bag; he was very tired.

To our amazement, the store was busy; we realized it was probably due to the fact that the store was air-conditioned. It had a small café and bar at the back. There were no seats available as everyone was coming in to cool off with a cold drink. Our decisions were simple, stand at the small bar and have another drink, or wait for someone to leave a table. There were only four small round white wrought iron tables with small ornate chairs to match them.

There was very little choice of beer and they only had cans. The barmen had to run from the shop counter to the bar, since he was the only one working there. When he came over, he puts three cans on the counter and told us that was all he had, and asked what brand we wanted. We choose the Heineken, as it was the only brand that we were familiar with. As he handed us the beers, he pointed to a table where a young couple were leaving. We could see from the window, the Acropolis, illuminated in the night sky. The cold Heineken was a pleasant change after the walk from the restaurant.

It was after ten thirty, and there was no sign of the store closing. Before we finished our beer, the barman asked if we wanted another. We figured that we should get the cold drinks and head back to our tents.

The person running the establishment seemed to be in no hurry to close. I pointed to my watch and asked when he closed up, and he replied that was whenever the last customer left. His partner opened up at 8.00 in the morning, and with the unusual heat we had now, people came to cool off and buy drinks

I asked if he served any breakfast here. He said he most certainly did; we have coffee, tea, croissants and a selection of pastries. We can cook a breakfast if you pre order. Most of the campers take out what they want and cook it themselves. We asked for eggs and bacon with croissants, two coffees and one tea. "Please reserve a table with three chairs for 8.30 am. If you can give us a receipt, we will pay now."

He replied, "You are on the campsite, all you have to do sign the bill and I will add it to your account if you like." We told him that we preferred to pay now for our beers, and keep breakfast separate. He was fine with that. We finished our beers, bought some cans of ginger ale and left for our tents.

As we were heading to our tents, I was not sure what time we would be able to get Brian up. We were sure of having breakfast in an air-conditioned café, and I knew that this would please him after such a warm night. Approaching the tents, we could hear Brian snoring; he was sound asleep. Since he was asleep now, we should have no trouble getting him up early for breakfast in a cool place.

We pulled our sleeping bags out and lay on them next to the car so when the sun came up, it would not shine on us, and hopefully we would wake up in the shade. The night is almost unbearable with the humidity, I slept soundly for about three hours; I woke up sweating and just dozed for an hour or two until the sun came up. I got up and went straight to the showers with my kit bag to cool down and clean up.

It was six o'clock and the shower block was very quiet. It was a super clean and modern facility; easily the best I have been in since we left home and travelled across Europe. There was no air-conditioning, but it was extremely well ventilated with fans turning near openings at the top of the walls.

There was only one young fellow in there; a very pleasant young man from the USA. He mentioned that he was from Florida and was accustomed to this warm, humid weather. He and his girlfriend had been in Greece for a week, and they were staying on this campsite. They were enjoying all the museums and the sights very much.

I headed back at about 6.45, I saw Tony walking towards me, he told me Brian was up and would have a shower so that he would be on time to come with us for breakfast. He was glad that we had booked a table. The temperature was climbing fast, and the pool was open with people already swimming at seven in the morning.

Before I could reach the tents, Brian passed me and with a big grin on his face, and said, "good morning Alan, see you at breakfast." I knew he would be pleased, as we needed to make an early start. What is better than breakfast in a cool spot before starting out. On our last day together we would hopefully complete all the paper work, and buy the ticket for him to fly out as soon as possible.

Breakfast at the camp store was quite an experience; Brian was very impressed with the ocean view from the back window. We could not see the Acropolis, but it was a great view of some ancient parts of the city. Our power breakfast was extremely good; eggs, bacon, tomatoes and nice brown toast. We had our usual, fresh coffee and Brian enjoyed his tea. We were having a very relaxing breakfast. This was a wonderful start to the day.

Tony decided to come with us in case we needed him to stay in the car while we dealt with the ownership transfer. We had the car right outside the store, so we were able to head straight to the garage to talk to the dealer. The garage wasn't far, and we hoped we didn't have one-way street problems.

Arriving at the dealership, we saw the man waiting for us. He told us to leave the car, lock it and come with him; he will drive us to the transfer office. It would be a lot easier because he knew his way around, and as an added plus he had air conditioning in his car.

When we arrived at the transfer office, we were told that we needed a solicitor's affidavit stating that the ownership could be transferred. They also needed to have witnessed proof, so we had to go to see a lawyer.

Ray, the dealer knew a lawyer, as obviously he has done this before. We went to this lawyer's office, as it was fairly close to the garage. This would be easy to achieve, but we might have to wait if he was very busy. Brian was concerned, and asked Ray how much this was going to cost, as lawyers were expensive. Ray confirmed that his friend would do the work for 20 drachma. "That is a lot of money." Brian stated, and Ray said "do you want to sell the car?" Brian very calmly said, "Yes, sorry, let's get this completed."

When we were parked outside the lawyer's office, Ray asked Tony to stay in the car, and drive it around the block if we didn't return in one hour, as parking was limited and expensive. The office was two flights of stairs up, and I was concerned about Brian climbing the long flights of stairs but he said "I will be fine."

Reaching the lawyer's office, the secretary told us to go right in. There were rows of books on one wall and large oil paintings on the other, the office was very large, and air conditioned. Ray spoke in Greek to the man standing behind his desk. We all shook hands and he soon had some paperwork ready for me to sign. It was very simple process, pay a small fee, sign, and we're done.

Ray said, "now all we have to do is hope when we get to the transfer office, it is quiet and there is no waiting. Hopefully we can get all this completed, and be back to our campsite by midday. Upon arrival at the office our wish was answered, it was very quiet and everything was competed with a minimum of fuss. Ray now owns the car. We breathed a sigh of relief.

Brian was satisfied that he now had an additional amount of cash to add to his already large funds. Ray asked other than the campsite, where we would like to go, as he could help us out. He was happy to help us out since he got such a great deal on the car. I suggested he take us to a store where I could buy a backpack and then to a travel agency. Brian thought that was a good request and Ray took us to a very large market with a travel agency right outside the market entrance.

When he dropped us off at the market, Brian saw the travel agent to ask about a ticket to Tehran, the young lady behind the desk asked him when he wanted to fly out, because there was a great deal on a flight today. This was just the answer Brian wanted, he asked how much, knowing he would take it.

We left with Brian and went into the market to buy my backpack as promised. I found a green canvas and wicker one that was very unusual, but I liked it; and he bought it for me. We now had to get a taxi back to the campsite as Brian was flying out in the afternoon. The cab ride to the campsite was very short, and Brian packed quickly while the cab waited. He wanted us to come to the airport with him; he would pay for the cab ride both ways.

We were not really very interested in going, but Tony said yes we would come and bid him farewell. We had enjoyed most of the adventure, even if we did not reach his intended destination. The ride to the airport was approximately twenty minutes and Brian kept his word and paid for the cab back to the campsite for us.

I took his case out, shook his hand and told him to be careful and only use the money daily that he had in his pocket. He smiled and said, "I understand what you are saying." He was aware, that we now knew his shoulder bag was full of cash. He disappeared into the airport and Tony and I were free to explore Greece and find our way home.

The cash he gave us was enough for the cab back with a little left for us to enjoy drink. We would plan our trip later.

CHAPTER 29

As we arrived at the Athena campsite, I suggested to Tony that we go into the camp store and have a cold beer as a celebration. We had a cold beer and found it so relaxing to just sit there, and have nothing to worry about. This was something we looked forward to, as the huge responsibility of the car, and looking after Brian was now finally over. Our long adventure had become more torture than pleasure.

I wondered if we could head back in the direction of Vienna, so somehow I could see Lisa. I remembered that I had cards to mail her and my parents. When I mentioned this to Tony, his answer was "You will have to make that journey to Vienna on your own, because I plan on going to the Acropolis, then spend some time relaxing on a Greek island. You should realize that to travel from here to Austria will not be easy as it's not a very direct route." His plan was to find a ferry from there to an island, then up to Corfu. From Corfu there was a ferry to Brindisi in Italy, and a bus through Rome and back to Paris.

"That sounds like a good plan, I will join you, but I do not have a great amount of funds. Lisa can wait." "Great, I have plenty of funds and can lend you some money to get home. You can pay me back later."

"Thanks you're a real friend, I'm now confident we'll have a good time visiting the Greek islands, and getting home safely."

Brian had paid the campsite bill for one more night, so we had to pack and head out of there in the morning. Our plan was to locate a transit bus to get us to the Acropolis the next day, and from there, we would investigate what our options were for the cheapest way to reach the island ferries.

The morning air was very warm, and as usual I got up at six. Our breakfast was rivita (large dry Swedish whole-wheat cracker) with peanut butter and coffee. Tony said, "We will be having whatever we have left to eat from now on, and quite often it may be dry bread and warm water." This is an inexpensive life when one is on the road on a tight budget. There were no real luxuries from here as we wanted to travel as cheaply as possible, and only take transportation when necessary.

Our plan for the day was to investigate the best route to the Acropolis, and where to pick up a ferry to the islands. As we packed up the tent, I was so glad that I now had a backpack and a suitcase so I could travel "in style." I had to decide on what to do with the case, clothes and especially the transistor radio that had been our only real contact with the outside world. They all were too heavy to carry, travelling to the islands and walking on beaches.

As we left the campsite we were approached by a young Australian man and his friend. He asked, "What's in the suitcase, not enough room in your pack mate?" We laughed and told him of our travels over the past two weeks.

"We may be able to help, let's have a coffee in the store," he said. While we sat in the cool café having a fresh coffee, he introduced himself as Gary and his girlfriend as Sue. They had a camper van and were heading back for Southern England. I asked if they would take my case to my home in England, and in return they could have the radio and spare batteries.

They were very happy to do this, and asked where in England I wanted the case to go. I explained that my parent's house was only four miles from Southampton, and that was where they would be crossing the channel to England. They were glad to do it; I gave them my home address and my parents' names, I also gave them my case, and the radio, as promised. They were very interested in meeting my mother and father and telling them of my and travels.

When we left, we wished them an enjoyable and safe journey to England. We also advised them about the roads in Yugoslavia, which we took. They were both young and extremely adventurous. We explained all about the roads we had taken, and this made them even more excited about trying to find them and travel back as much as possible on the route we took.

I was walking to the bus station in downtown Athens, and thinking how it was so much easier without a heavy case. When we reached the crowded station, we sat on a non air cooled bus with our packs on our laps, so we could get a seat. The distance from the campsite to this famous tourist attraction was very deceptive. From the store at night with all the flood lights, it did not look very far. When the small city bus finally stopped, we had to wait for most of the people to get off and give us room to manoeuvre our backpacks.

When clear of the bus, we looked up the path to the world famous site. I was a little disappointed, as it was a lot smaller structure than I imagined it. The site was well worth visiting, despite my initial observation. We wandered around with our backpacks; we saw that there were many back packers from all parts of the world. After walking around for two hours, we decided to go back to downtown Athens, and to the docks.

In order to get to the ferries to the islands, we had to take a long bus ride from Athens. We looked at the map and chose to go to the Island of Salamina. People had mentioned it had small, quaint fishing villages with some very quiet beaches, which were not commercialised. The bus ride back was a lot more comfortable, as there were less people

We hopped on a bus right to the ferry terminal at Pireas, the port for Athens. This was a well spread out docking facility. It had a lot of ferries with many destinations to all the islands. At last, we found the right dock and after a short wait our boat came in. The ferry to Salamina was a small one and was not too expensive. The brief journey provided a picturesque vista of the clear blue, calm sea.

We arrived on the island and found only inexpensive and small mini buses for transportation. The island was large, and we needed to get a bus to the other side to find the deserted beach areas that we wanted to explore. We asked the bus drivers, and tried to find out which one would get us to the quiet side of the island. One driver, to whom we showed the map, told us, he could help us. We jumped on a bus and joined some locals. We assumed we are heading where we wanted to go. After a very rough ride on some bad roads, we were at our destination.

We exited at a small village with no sign of a beach or water. We were now in the middle of the island and completely lost. The bus had gone; and we walked into the village. It had rows of white, one-storey houses, with shutters on the small windows, and red tiled roofs. As we wandered down the short street, it looked like a ghost town, as there wasn't a soul in site. Later we found out that it was deserted at midday, as it was the home of many Athenians who commuted to work from Salamina.

We were hoping to find a café, as we were absolutely parched, so we walked along the main street of this village. We looked down each side street and hoped to find a café or shop to buy a drink. We had no luck; we walked back to where we got off the bus, and waited under the only tree there, seeking some shade from the blistering heat and humidity of the afternoon.

After almost an hour the bus returned, and we paid our fare and went back to the docks, where we found a fellow backpacker who helped us decide where we should go next. We chose to go back to the mainland and find a ferry that would take us to the Ionian island of Corfu, the scene of the Odyssee. Colonial Britain had built a cemetery, estates, architectural gardens, a fortress and a banknote museum there.

At the docks we went into a bar for a cold beer and met a Swiss backpacker who told us he had been to Corfu or Kerkira. Among the tangle of narrow alleyways, he had found shuttered Venetian buildings and two castles at strategic locations enclosed by the capital. He described it as a small paradise on earth, as the scenery changed without affecting the harmony of the terrain. The flower-strewn countryside and Adriatic-style villages, also made us want to go this popular tourist destination. On the southwest coast of the island, there was a beautiful deserted beach, as well as caves. There was also a nude beach. He had been there for a week and was heading home now after travelling through Europe for ten months.

He continued to tell us, "The beach is about four miles long. When you reach it, there are steep sandy cliffs on each side of an opening looking out on the Adriatic Sea. This is the only access onto this beach, you go to your left, and set up your tent well away from the access. If you walk about halfway along, you're right at the middle point."

Pausing, he said, "On the weekends, the locals come down, and I was told they did not like strangers around their children. They consider it their private spot even though it's not. The bus will take you to a village called Mathias; it stops at a small lane that leads to the village, and you have to walk from there. Make sure you have plenty of water with you as it's a long walk, about 3 miles to the beach, and the road is very rough. There is a water tap at the entrance to the beach that I used while I was there."

"Passing through the village, you will see olive groves and some orange trees. There is a very small store with a village café that looks like it really is someone's dining room. They cook a tasty evening meal for anyone who wants to eat there. The store is very basic, you can get regular food items very cheaply there, and you will find the local people very friendly."

Because he recognized my accent, he asked what part of England I was from. When I answered Southampton, he asked me about the Saint's football club.

As we left the bar, he pointed to a large car ferry and said that one would take us to Corfu, if we hurry, as it was leaving soon. It was a six hour long trip, and it wouldn't be back until the next day. There were only two runs daily.

We thanked him for his information, and we hurried to buy our tickets for the ferry, and quickly boarded it. The ferry was almost the size of the one we came over from Southampton to France on. We headed for the bar which was our saving grace in the heat. We were going to be on board for the rest of the day, so we made ourselves comfortable for the humid trip to Corfu. With its winding streets and narrow alleyways, this cosmopolitan city was surrounded by lush vegetation and gentle slopes.

This was a beautiful pub, with lots of glass and mirrors, a huge selection of spirits which were well displayed at the back. There were also pumps on the bar so they had draught beer as well. This was not a lounge you would expect to see on a ferry.

The barman was from the Caribbean and spoke English well. He greeted us, saying, "Good afternoon gentleman, we have a nice selection of cold beers and I'm sure we'll have a beer for you, maybe a Stella? We smiled and said, "Yes, two please."

He was interested in where we were from, and where we were we going, as he has had lots of backpackers in the bar from all parts of the world. We told him that we were heading for a quiet beach area in Southern Corfu. It was not a place he was be familiar with, but sounded like an area he would like to check out when he had the time. He had a small off road motorcycle, and that would be a perfect place for him to visit.

We sat at a table by the window, and we saw people with their vehicles coming aboard. The bar area was deserted, so we chose the most comfortable spot for our voyage. We asked the bar keeper if we could stay there for the duration of the passage, and asked when he closed the bar. He replied, "The bar is always open, and it has been very quiet for the last week or so, please sit and enjoy."

Tony got out his travelling chess set; it was so small that we could play anywhere. I was not a good player myself, but the few times I had played, Tony had taught me.

We soon felt the ferry shudder and shake; we knew we were on our way. We played two games of chess, and each had a couple of beers. This made the time pass very quickly. The route did not take us out of the sight of land, as we could always see the coast line.

The bar was now more than half full. Many people did not even have drinks; they just sat near the windows enjoying the picturesque views of the coast line, which at times was so close, that we could see people and cars on the roads.

After our games of chess, we put our feet on our packs and dozed off for a while. The barman woke us when we were about fifteen minutes from docking. We had slept for two hours, and we were now the only two people in the bar. Everyone else was lining up to get off.

There was no rush for us, since we had to wait until after the ferry docked. We put our packs on our backs when most of the crowd had cleared. It was easier to move around with less people. I had to get used to the idea that when you turned around with a backpack, you could hit people if you didn't look behind you.

It was early evening, as we left the ferry docks, and we were looking for a place to sleep the night. Many backpackers were heading in different directions. We stopped and asked a small group of people if they were also looking for a campsite. A very cute young blonde said "sure, follow us we have been told there is a good one this way, and it is only a twenty minute walk from here."

She was fascinated with my English accent, and wanted to know about where we were from. Smiling, she mentioned that there was sound and music show tonight, and they were all going; we should join them after we set up our tents at the campsite.

The campsite was very nice, and there were all tents, and no camper vans. It was small with adequate facilities; that were all we needed for the night. We weren't too sure about going to the show, as we wanted to get a good night's sleep; and get an early bus to our planned remote beach adventure.

There was a small café right outside the campsite, and we went there for something to eat after we set up Tony's small tent. The young girl saw us and waved, then pointing to her watch, indicated the show was on after ten. That convinced us that it would be way too late an evening. We decided to eat and go back to the campsite to sleep, as soon as the sun went down. The evening was cooler; it was probably close to 20c, so we would have a good night's sleep.

The small café was reasonably priced and served typical Greek local food, basically fish or lamb stew. There were about ten small round black wooden tables, and plain white painted stone walls; material was draped on them to compliment large wooden statues on the floor. The statutes were painted, but were so old that the paint was chipping off. The ceiling was an old fishing net with the lights coming through, which made for an unusual lighting effect.

There was no menu, just a chalk board with the food cooked that day. We ordered the fish fries with "chips" and, of course a Greek salad. We had never eaten potatoes the way they made them, but they were really great. It was an excellent restaurant.

I thought about Lisa, and felt I that must send her a postcard soon. I knew that it would not be long before we would head home, and I would be able to see her again; thinking about that uplifted my spirits.

CHAPTER 30

The night was cool. We never realized that the sound and light show was so close, it was in the castle grounds right next to the campsite. Although we did not get a solid night's sleep due to the noise, we still got up early, washed, packed up and headed for the bus station. There were not many buses running on the island: there were just a few main roads.

We went into a rustic looking café right beside the bus depot and had a light breakfast. We ordered brown toast, fried eggs and fresh coffee. The bus we needed had left very early, and the next one was not for an hour.

The bus ride took us through some wide open areas with fields, but no houses or signs of life. We exited the bus at our stop; and found this area was remote, and that this was the road that would take us through the village to the beach we were told about. The road was straight and led us right into the village. The buildings were very old and looked like they were in need of repair.

People smiled and waved as we walked through the village, and children began following us. A dog was barking; we saw that he was tied up in front of a house. There was no grass around the houses, and only dirt pathways between them. The road turned into a track, and we had to walk carefully between the deep, dried out tire tracks. This town looked like it had not seen rain for some time.

We looked straight ahead of us, and all we could see were the ever present olive trees. It was a sweltering heat. We hoped it wasn't too far to the beach, and that the water in our canteens would last. The fact that we could swim when we got there kept us motivated. The opening in the clay like cliffs could be seen in the distance, an estimated two miles away.

As we reached the beach, it was just as we had been told, totally desolate and not a soul in sight. We decided to go right on to the beach, which ran in a northerly direction, and was bounded by low clay cliffs. The clean white sand was very hot on our feet, even with sandals on. We almost sank into the sand with our heavy packs on our backs. A little way from the sand, we found a firm path between a few rocks, and decided to stay there for a while. We went in for a swim to cool off from the blistering sun. It was over thirty Celsius.

It was late afternoon and as the sun went down the temperature dropped a little, but it was still very warm, so we decided to roll out our sleeping bags and sleep in the open on the deserted beach for the night. During the night, the temperature dropped, and it became a lot cooler than we expected, so we slept in our sleeping bags and had a restful sleep.

We woke up early to see the sun rising. It was very pleasant; however, the beach was unexpectedly busy, as we could see animal tracks all around us along the sand. One set of winding string like lines went between us and on to the beach. When we realized that it was a snake track, we figured this was not a good part of the beach to sleep on.

Since we didn't have much food with us we thought, after our morning swim we would head back up to the village to get some breakfast. On the track back we met a local young man on a small motorcycle. He stopped to say good morning, and seemed very surprised to find people in such an isolated area so early in the day. His English was excellent and he seemed to be a very amicable person. We asked him if knew of anywhere in the village where we could get something to eat.

"Sure there is a very small café which looks like a store, you cannot miss it. Halfway up the street on the right, you will see a gathering point for everyone in the village, and they will be very happy to see you, as they do not get a lot of tourist's here."

He asked us where we slept last night, and when we said on the beach, he was shocked and asked if we were in a tent. When we told him we slept in the open, he asked if we saw any animals, because at night when it was cooler, some creatures moved along parts of the beach. You saw their tracks in the sand the next morning.

When I explained about the tracks, he suggested that if we planned on sleeping there again, we should go left in the southerly direction, as we would be much safer there. He advised us to keep well away from the main opening to the beach, as the locals came down some afternoons with their children. They were a little uneasy with strangers on their beach. He advised us to walk about a mile south and we would be fine there. We thanked him for this valuable information, and we headed up to the village.

When we arrived at the village, breakfast was the first thing on our minds. We had seen and heard chickens, so we assumed the local village café would have some eggs and toast. There were people sitting on their front steps drinking coffee, and watching their children running around and enjoying themselves. The village seemed very alive for this early in the morning.

It was extremely warm and dry, as we trod along a dusty road. We hoped for calm, because if it got windy, it would be an absolute dust bowl.

Upon entering the café, we saw it was full of locals. They were extremely polite; two men offered us their table. A young man, who spoke English well, came to us and asked if we would like tea or coffee. There was no menu, he just asked, "would eggs and toast be alright?" We thought that sounded like a good idea. He returned with a teapot and two mugs, and we enjoyed our drinks while waiting for our morning meal.

The café was a rough old place with a plain wooden floor, a few thread bear carpets, stone walls with very small windows and a few lights that were hanging on long wires from a fairly high ceiling. It had light bulbs without lampshades. It was very tidy and clean. The tables and chairs were painted light brown with streaks of different colours in them. I would imagine that they had mixed up whatever paints they had, but not too well, and this gave the chairs and tables a unique look of 'art deco.'

Our breakfast arrived and it was mouth-watering, three eggs each, fried tomatoes, potatoes and some fine brown toast. This was a breakfast fit for a king or queen. It was a startling amount of food, which would certainly keep us going for the day.

The atmosphere was friendly, and even though we were young holiday backpackers, the old folks accepted that, and were really nice to us. Some people looked and were very curious of young fellows entering their space for a short period. This was a place that had not seen too many travellers, because the rough track was only good for motorcycles and trucks with very stable ground clearance.

After we paid our bill for breakfast, we headed back to the beach. The walk back was not as hard on us as the day before, when we walked in the immense heat. Our plan was to walk south on the beach and find a good spot to pitch the tent away from the wildlife.

As we reached the beach, it became quite warm. Walking on the sand was very uncomfortable, so we had to walk in the water on firmer sand. The beach was about two miles long. At a rocky point, we decided to pitch our tent midway between it and the opening where we came in. The sandy cliff was about 100 feet high at the back of the beach, and about 35 yards wide in some places.

We didn't want to be too close to the cliff, so we set up our camp about forty feet out from it. We set up our tent, and the fly sheet from the tent set, close to our supplies. We were confident in this remote area; we would not have any visitors. With our camp area set, we went into the sea for a swim to cool off.

That evening we walked up to the village for a hot meal and a cold beer. That was our regular routine for the week that we were there. After supper we always headed for our tent. Tony read, while I wrote in my journal. After several days of relaxing in this idealistic setting, we decided it was time to return to our normal daily lives.

After a good night's sleep, we made our way back up the track, early the next morning while it was cool. We weren't sure what time the bus would come, so we decided to walk, or hitch a ride with whoever came along. After walking for a while on this very quiet road, a priest stopped his car and asked where we were going. We told him we needed a ride to the ferry port. The Dutch priest told us he could drop us off there. He was intrigued with our story of how we came to be on the beach, past the village, in this extremely remote area.

CHAPTER 31

On our arrival at the port in Corfu Town in Greece, the Dutch priest informed us the ferry leaving shortly was going to Brindisi, Italy. He took us right up to the ticket office, and told us to have a safe trip home. We purchased our tickets without any problem, and thanks to our early arrival, we were able to catch the first ferry of the day. There were only two crossings each day, and it was nice to get the first one, as our journey home to England was going to be long. It was pleasant to cruise up the Adriatic Sea in daylight. The ferry was crowded, and this was the first time I had seen a swimming pool on a ferry.

When we left the port, the wind was blowing hard, and the sea was rough. There were a number of people around the pool, and some were in it. The water was slapping from side to side as the ship lurched up and down. It was not long before they announced that the pool would be closing as the sea was too rough. In the lounge, we found some comfortable reclining chairs and played cards to pass the time as this passage was going to take most of the day.

Tony suggested that one of us go and get something to eat while the other kept our seats, as it was getting cloudy out, and people would be coming into the lounge. There was no sun for them to tan. Our decision on who would go for the food would be made by playing a game of checkers. I won and decided to stay with our seats. Tony suggested he get a meat sandwich or a burger, if there was any, and he knew my choice was always a cheeseburger.

Almost an hour had passed, and I was getting concerned. A few minutes later he arrived with a cheeseburger for each of us, and a two bottles of beer. He said he was delayed as the line ups in the cafeteria were ridiculous, probably the longest he had ever seen on a ferry. There was only one more choice of where to eat and that was the restaurant, but we would have lost our comfy seats in the lounge, so Tony had patiently waited in line.

There was a tremendous amount of people onboard, and the ferry was very close to capacity, or even over. I checked the number of life boats, and looking at people aboard, I was quite concerned, travelling on the rough Adriatic Sea. When we arrived in Brindisi, we decided to wait in the lounge until most of the passengers had disembarked, as moving in crowds with a backpack on a ship was not easy.

We left the ferry in mid-afternoon, and we asked port officials where the bus terminal was, so we could catch a bus north into Western Europe. It was right outside the port. The place was crowded and it was a real task moving around. We purchased tickets for the coach leaving at 5.30 pm. that would take us to Rome and Paris. We played chess and ate while we waited.

The modern coach was lacking a washroom and air conditioning, so it was not too comfortable. We managed to get our packs stored in cabinets under the bus, as we were on board for the complete trip, while a lot of passengers were getting off before we reached France. For the first two hours we had to contend with a screaming baby, and when it got quieter, we fell asleep.

Our first stop at seven-thirty was amusing, as we had no experience with European highway rest stops. In Italy, we only had twenty minutes. It was absolutely unbelievable to us to have so many people on this stopover. We had a limited time to go to the washrooms and get back to our seats. There were line ups, lots of pushing and shoving and arguing. The driver was very strict and made it clear when we stopped that he would leave in twenty minutes as he had a tight schedule to keep to. If one was not back on board, they had to get the next bus.

We traveled at at night on the warm coach, it was cosy and quiet as most people were trying to sleep. We tried to do the same, but it was so humid that it was not easy. As we passed through Rome late at night, we could see some well lit up old buildings. We passed Florence and Milan; we continued following the mountains, and it became cooler. We traveled through the Mount Blanche Tunnel which was 6.5 miles long was quite thrilling. This connection between France and Italy greatly shortened our travel time. At 15, 800 feet high, it is the second highest point in the Alps. The alpine scenery on both sides of the tunnel, and throughout the mountains and valleys was breathtaking; lots of snow could be seen on the mountains. The cable cars and ski lifts were easily visible. As we descended, the temperature rose slightly. There was a delay at customs at the French-Italian border. We were now running late and the driver was on edge, and he seemed to be travelling a lot faster as we continued in an effort to make up time and keep to schedule. At this sped by, we saw little in the dark.

Our next rest stop was Geneva, Switzerland. It is an international city near France, where the League of Nations was and the Red

Cross is now. We were 40 minutes behind schedule, so our stop which was supposed to be one hour was cut in half. It was not a busy place, and everything was expensive. The rush to get food and use the washrooms was not as great. We managed to buy a quick meal and drink in the time allowed; we hurried back to the coach. As we continued, the driver again was barrelling along at a great rate on the divided highway to Paris.

We arrived in Paris about two am, and we walked around this lovely city to pass the time and see what we could, since the Metro (underground rail system) did not open until 5.30 am. The Paris Underground was the cheapest transport for getting us to the railway station, where we could get a train up to a ferry port, and cross the English Channel for home. A café opened at five, and we had a toasted sausage and cheese sandwich with coffee.

After walking up the Champs Ellysees, we saw the Arc de Triomphe, and walked down and along the Seine River to the Eiffel Tower, we were anxious to get going. We finally chose a different coach ride to the coast, as it was the least expensive way out of Paris. The bus was leaving right away, the time difference between the cities was not a factor, as the train didn't go into Dieppe.

CHAPTER 32

We disembarked at the Dieppe Terminal, got a ferry across the channel to Dover, and then took the train to Waterloo Station in London. This was where Tony and exchanged phone numbers, and said goodbye for a while.

Buying a ticket for the last part of the ride home to Southampton was easy. I had done it many times. The train left almost right away from a nearby platform. The hour and a half train ride home to Southampton was very fast but was a bumpy ride, trying to eat something on the train was a real hardship.

After a short walk from the railway station to the bus depot, I was lucky to get a bus ride within a short distance of my parent's village. The walk home would take me over an hour, but I knew I would surely find my mum and dad home. They would be very pleased to have their traveller back. I knew I would not need my key, as I could just walk in the back door and they would be in the kitchen or in the back yard.

Walking along the lane to my house was an exciting feeling, because I remembered dad's last words to me as I was about to drive away, (Please come home safe son.) These words have remained with me to this day. My father was not an emotional man, and for me to hear those words from him was like he said, "I love you very much and want to see you again." I was looking forward to seeing the look on his face, and giving my mum a big hug.

When I opened the kitchen door and walked in, it was just as I expected, dad's comment was the wanderer returns, with hug from mum and firm hand shake from dad. My father said, "Let us have cup of tea and let me tell you about the detective who came to see us the day after you left." I was intrigued and extremely interested to know what happened.

"Well son, the man you travelled with was a criminal on the run. He was a fraudulent man with a number of bank accounts. For each of these he had a cheque book and a bank cheque card, which would allow him to draw about L50 sterling daily from most of the banks in Europe. (The UK police force) Scotland Yard assumed he would accumulate enough money in Europe to get through to the Middle East. This would mean he had to get to as many banks as possible each day and change currency as he passed through each country. So he would not be sightseeing, but concentrating on this objective, lest he run out of funds and get stranded. Surely he could not turn to the embassy, consulate or local police, if he got in trouble. The other important thing you should know is he has also committed some indecent acts with young boys or girls and is considered a dangerous paedophile and a wanted criminal.

Next, he asked, "can your son take care of himself? "I told him that, "if you caught him with a boy, you would most certainly beat him severely, even though you were normally a very calm chap. Such acts would make his blood boil. And the old fellow would have no chance. I gave my son lessons in boxing when he was only eleven. I have only seen Alan having a problem with a number of young men on one occasion. The bullies were all given a lesson from him, so believe me he can take care of himself very well if the occasion presents itself."

The officer then told us that if we received any correspondence from Mr. Turner, to please inform them, as they were trying to track his whereabouts. "Our concern was for you and how you could get involved in this, and were you in any danger. My dad told him I did not have a clue; I was innocent of the whole situation, and did not do anything wrong. He is therefore not an accomplice, so he can relax."

To this date we have not heard anything else from him, so who knows what happened. I just knew that I was one lucky guy, who had an unforgettable journey with unexpected events that were handled well.

This journey was an interesting one and we did enjoy ourselves. I had written a daily journal, and that was how this story describing events that took place came about.

CPSIA information can be obtained at www.ICGtesting.com
Printed in the USA
LVOW060857090812

293538LV00003B/2/P